First World War

and Army of Occupation

War Diary

France, Belgium and Germany

28 DIVISION
83 Infantry Brigade
King's Own (Yorkshire Light Infantry)
1st Battalion
8 November 1914 - 31 October 1915

WO95/2274/1

The Naval & Military Press Ltd
www.nmarchive.com
Published in association with The National Archives

Published by

The Naval & Military Press Ltd

Unit 10 Ridgewood Industrial Park,

Uckfield, East Sussex,

TN22 5QE England

Tel: +44 (0) 1825 749494

www.naval-military-press.com

www.nmarchive.com

This diary has been reprinted in facsimile from the original. Any imperfections are inevitably reproduced and the quality may fall short of modern type and cartographic standards.

Contents

Document type	Place/Title	Date From	Date To
Heading	WO95/2274/1		
Heading	28th Division 83rd Infy Bde 1st Bn K.O.Y.L.I. Nov 1914-Oct 1915 From:- Straits Settlements to Salonika		
Heading	83rd Bde. 28th Div. War Diary 1st K.O.Y.L.I. November December 1914 Oct 15		
Miscellaneous	1st. Bn. The King's Own Yorkshire Light Infantry	12/07/1915	12/07/1915
War Diary	Southampton	08/11/1914	08/11/1914
War Diary	Hursley Park	08/11/1914	16/11/1914
War Diary	Harwich	17/11/1914	21/12/1914
War Diary	Hursley Park	23/12/1914	30/12/1914
Heading	83rd Bde. 28th Div. War Diary 1st K.O.Y.L.I. January 1915		
War Diary	Winchester	01/01/1915	15/01/1915
War Diary	Havre	16/01/1915	17/01/1915
War Diary	Hazebrouck	18/01/1915	18/01/1915
War Diary	Oultersteene	18/01/1915	29/01/1915
Heading	83rd Bde. 28th Div. War Diary 1st K.O.Y.L.I. February 1915		
War Diary	Oultersteene	01/02/1915	02/02/1915
War Diary	Ypres-Comines	02/02/1915	08/02/1915
War Diary	Ouderdom	11/02/1915	15/02/1915
War Diary	Ypres	15/02/1915	21/02/1915
War Diary	Ouderdom	26/02/1915	28/02/1915
Diagram etc			
Miscellaneous	A Form. Messages And Signals		
Diagram etc	Scale 1/10000		
Heading	83rd Bde. 28th Div. War Diary Attached With Bde. To 5th Div. From 3rd March. 1st K.O.Y.L.I. March 1915		
War Diary		01/03/1915	03/03/1915
War Diary	Bailleul	11/03/1915	29/03/1915
Miscellaneous			
Diagram etc	Sketch Map Dranoutre Section		
Heading	83rd Bde. 25th Div. War Diary Returned With Bde. From 5th Div. 6.4.15. 1st K.O.Y.L.I. April 1915		
Heading	1/K.O.Y.L.I. 2-30 April 1915		
War Diary	Aldershot Camp Neuve Eglise	02/04/1915	02/04/1915
War Diary	Boeschepe	07/04/1915	09/04/1915
War Diary	Ypres	09/04/1915	16/04/1915
War Diary	Huts Between Ypres And Vlamertinghe	19/04/1915	30/04/1915
Heading	28th Division War Diary Of The 1st King's Own Yorkshire Light Infantry From 1-5-15 To 31-5-15 Volume V		
Heading	War Diary Of The 1st King's Own Yorkshire Light Infantry From 1-5-15 To 31-5-15 Volume V		
War Diary		01/05/1915	31/05/1915
Heading	83rd Bde. 28th Div. War Diary 1st K.O.Y.L.I. June 1915		
Heading	On His Majesty's Service.		
War Diary		01/06/1915	18/06/1915
War Diary	La Clytte	18/06/1915	19/06/1915

War Diary	Kemmel Bivouac	20/06/1915	30/06/1915
Heading	83rd Bde. 28th Div. War Diary 1st K.O.Y.L.I. July 1915		
Heading	On His Majesty's Service.		
War Diary	La Clytte	01/07/1915	04/07/1915
War Diary	Trenches	05/07/1915	11/07/1915
War Diary	La Clytte	12/07/1915	17/07/1915
War Diary	Trenches	18/07/1915	23/07/1915
War Diary	Scherpenberg	24/07/1915	30/07/1915
War Diary	Trenches	30/07/1915	31/07/1915
Miscellaneous	Remarks on Draft joined 20-8-15	20/08/1915	20/08/1915
Miscellaneous	No 15750 G.S.M.C. Corpse		
Miscellaneous	21991 G.		
Miscellaneous	M.O. 1st K.O.Y.L.I.	10/08/1915	10/08/1915
Miscellaneous	1st K.O.Y.L.I.	11/08/1915	11/08/1915
Miscellaneous	Remarks on Draft joined 5-8-15	05/08/1915	05/08/1915
Miscellaneous	To The Officer Commanding 1st Batt King's Own Lancashire Light Infantry	01/08/1915	01/08/1915
Diagram etc	Scale 1/5000		
Miscellaneous	Ref Map Sheet 28 Ypres		
Heading	83rd Bde. 28th Div. War Diary 1st K.O.Y.L.I. August 1915		
Heading	On His Majesty's Service.		
War Diary	Trenches	01/08/1915	06/08/1915
War Diary	Scherpenberg	07/08/1915	07/08/1915
War Diary	Trenches	12/08/1915	18/08/1915
War Diary	Scherpenberg	18/08/1915	24/08/1915
War Diary	Trenches	24/08/1915	30/08/1915
War Diary	Scherpenberg	31/08/1915	31/08/1915
Heading	83rd Bde. 28th Div. War Diary 1st K.O.Y.L.I. September 1915		
Heading	On His Majesty's Service.		
War Diary	Scherpenberg	01/09/1915	07/09/1915
War Diary	Trenches	07/09/1915	11/09/1915
War Diary	Schepenberg	12/09/1915	15/09/1915
War Diary	Trenches	17/09/1915	23/09/1915
War Diary	Outtersteene	24/09/1915	26/09/1915
War Diary	Robecq	27/09/1915	27/09/1915
War Diary	Noyelles Les Vermelles	28/09/1915	29/09/1915
War Diary	Trenches	29/09/1915	30/09/1915
Miscellaneous	Information Concerning Men of Draft Which joined 1st K.O.Y.L.I. 15th Sept 1915	15/09/1915	15/09/1915
Miscellaneous	C Form (Original). Messages And Signals		
Miscellaneous	C Form (Duplicate). Messages And Signals		
Miscellaneous	A Form. Messages And Signals		
Miscellaneous	C Form (Duplicate). Messages And Signals		
Miscellaneous	28th. Division Wire Begins	25/09/1915	25/09/1915
Miscellaneous	C Form (Duplicate). Messages And Signals		
Miscellaneous	C Form (Original). Messages And Signals		
Miscellaneous	C Form (Duplicate). Messages And Signals		
Miscellaneous	A Form. Messages And Signals		
Miscellaneous	1st King's Own Yorkshire Light Infantry	14/09/1915	14/09/1915
Miscellaneous	B.M.A. 560 Officer Commanding K.O.Y.L.I.	25/09/1915	25/09/1915
Heading	83rd Bde. 28th Div. War Diary Moved With Division To Salonika In November. 1st K.O.Y.L.I. October 1915		
War Diary	Trenches	01/10/1915	01/10/1915

War Diary	Annequin	02/10/1915	03/10/1915
War Diary	Trenches	03/10/1915	06/10/1915
War Diary	Gonnehem	07/10/1915	15/10/1915
War Diary	Le Quesnoy	16/10/1915	17/10/1915
War Diary	Trenches	18/10/1915	21/10/1915
War Diary	Cense La Vallee	22/10/1915	31/10/1915
Miscellaneous	A Form. Messages And Signals		
Miscellaneous	C Form (Triplicate). Messages And Signals		
Miscellaneous	Extract From The London Logette	04/10/1915	04/10/1915
Miscellaneous	A Form. Messages And Signals		

28TH DIVISION
83RD INFY BDE

1ST BN K.O.Y.L.I.

NOV ~~DEC~~ 1914-OCT 1915

FROM:- STRAITS SETTLEMENTS

TO SALONIKA

83rd Bde.

28th Div.

WAR DIARY

WAR DIARY

1st K. O. Y. L. I.

N O V E M B E R

D E C E M B E R

1 9 1 4

-----*-----

1

Oct 15

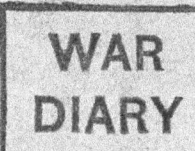

1st. Bn. THE KING'S OWN YORKSHIRE LIGHT INFANTRY.

Short History of the Battalion from August 1914.

83/8

Strength 33 Officers, 805 Other Ranks, including attached.

The majority of the men of the Battalion were recruited in South Yorkshire.

The Battalion was stationed in SINGAPORE on the outbreak of War, and left there 29th. September 1914 for England to form the 28th. Division which assembled a t WINCHESTER 23rd. December 1914. The Battalion was a unit of the 83rd. Brigade.

The Battalion embarked for FRANCE with the 28th. Division 15.1.15, and saw service in the YPRES salient until the beginning of March, when the 83rd. Brigade moved to the WULVERGHAM area, returning to the YPRES salient early in April.

The Battalion was present throughout the 2nd. Battle of YPRES.

On the 12th. May the Brigade were withdrawn and returned to the Salient 21st May until ~~3rd~~. June.

About the middle of June the Brigade took over the KEMMEL sector and remained there until 26th. September. The Battalion was present during this period.

On the 30th. September the Battalion moved down to LOOS with the Division and were in action for most of the period up to 23rd. October when the Division was withdrawn preparatory to moving to the East.

The Battalion embarked at MARSEILLES 25th. October 1915, and disembarked ALEXANDRIA 1st. November where ~~in~~ a month was spent refitting and resting.

The Battalion embarked 1st. December and disembarked at SALONICA 14th. December 1915.

Up to June 1st, 1916 the Battalion with the remainder of the Division was employed digging the Salonica Defence Line, making roads, and a small amount of training.

On June 4th the Battalion moved up country making roads and took over the Defence Line in the STRUMA VALLEY on July 15.1916.

The Battalion was engaged in the operations on the STRUMA PLAIN up to November 26th. The Battalion took an active part in the capture of BARAKLI DZUMA on 1st. October 1916.

On the 29th. November 1916, the Battalion, with the remainder of the 83rd. Brigade relieved an Italian Division and remainder there until April 29,1917.

From April 30, to 7th. June, the Battalion were in trenches in the DOIRAN SECTOR and returned to the STRUMA on the 19th. August 1917, and remained there until leaving the country 1st. July 1918.

During the period July 1916 to July 1918, the Battalion did a great deal of night patrol work on the STRUMA PLAIN, the patrols moving about 6000 yards out from the Outpost Line.

The Battalion suffered very heavily from Malaria and for eighteen months was considerably under strength.

The health of the Battalion ~~is~~, apart from Malaria is good. There are a great number of re-current malaria cases.

[illegible signature] Lt Col.

1st KING'S OWN YORKSHIRE LIGHT INFANTRY

Army Form C. 2118.

Instructions regarding War Diaries and Intelligence Summaries are contained in F. S. Regs., Part II. and the Staff Manual respectively. Title pages will be prepared in manuscript.

WAR DIARY
or
INTELLIGENCE SUMMARY.
(Erase heading not required.)

Place	Date	Hour	Summary of Events and Information	Remarks and references to Appendices

Hour, Date, Place	Summary of Events and Information	Remarks and references to App
4 p.m. 8.11.14 SOUTHAMPTON	Battalion arrived from [illegible] under command of Major [illegible] [illegible]	[illegible]
7 p.m. 8.11.14 HORSLEY PARK	Went into Camp	
11.30 a.m. 16.11.14 "	Orders received for the Battalion to proceed to [illegible]	[illegible]
4.30 p.m. 17.11.14 HARWICH	Arrived by train [illegible] [illegible] PARK [illegible]	[illegible]
9 a.m. 18.11.14 "	Took over [illegible] Transport	[illegible]
[illegible].12.14	[illegible] [illegible] Brooke [illegible] command [illegible]	[illegible]
7 a.m. 23.12.14 "	Entrained for [illegible] [illegible] PARK [illegible]	[illegible]
21.12.14 23.12.14 HORSLEY PARK	[illegible] [illegible] Battalion	[illegible]
24.12.14	The 6th Brigade assembled under command of [illegible]	[illegible]
[illegible]	[illegible]	[illegible]

D. D. & L., London, E.C.
(10340) Wt W5300/P713 750,000 3/18 E 2688 Forms C/2118/16.

83rd Bde.
28th Div.

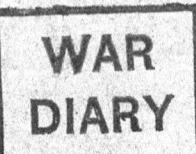

WAR
DIARY

1st K. O. Y. L. I.

J A N U A R Y

1 9 1 5

83rd Bde.
28th Division

Instructions regarding War Diaries and Intelligence Summaries are contained in F. S. Regs., Part II. and the Staff Manual respectively. Title pages will be prepared in manuscript.

WAR DIARY
or
INTELLIGENCE SUMMARY.
(Erase heading not required.)

Army Form C. 2118.

1st K.O.Y.L.I.

January 1915

Place	Date	Hour	Summary of Events and Information	Remarks and references to Appendices
	[illegible]		[illegible]	
			which [illegible] same day [illegible]	
			ESTER [illegible] in the [illegible]	
	5.1.15 10.1.15		A [illegible]	
	[illegible]		The 20th Division under the command of [illegible] was inspected by H.M. The Ki[illegible]	
	13.1.15		15 [illegible]	

200,000 (E) 8/14 J.B.C. & A. Forms/C. 2118/11
D. D. & L., London, E.C.
(10368) Wt W5300/P713 750,000 3/18 E 2688 Forms C/2118/16.

Instructions regarding War Diaries and Intelligence Summaries are contained in F. S. Regs., Part II. and the Staff Manual respectively. Title pages will be prepared in manuscript.

WAR DIARY
or
INTELLIGENCE SUMMARY.
(Erase heading not required.)

Army Form C. 2118.

Hour, Date, Place	Summary of Events and Information	Remarks and references to Appendices
7.45am 15.1.15 Winchester	Marched out for SOUTHAMPTON HRP	
12.30pm	Arrived SOUTHAMPTON DOCKS	
4pm	Sailed per S.S. BENARES HRP	
12 noon 16.1.15 HAVRE	Disembarked) HRP	
6.30am 17.1.15 HAVRE	Entrained) HRP	
5am 18.1.15 HAZEBROUCK	Arrived & detrained) HRP	
10.15am OULTERSTEENE	Went into Billets HRP	
12 noon 28.1.15 OULTERSTEENE	The 13th Brigade was inspected by the G.O.C. in Chi[illegible]	
11am 29.1.15 OULTERSTEENE	The 1st & 2nd Battalions met on the main road 2 Kilometres E. of BAILLEUL. The anniversary of SHINKIMAR [illegible]	

83rd Bde.
28th Div.

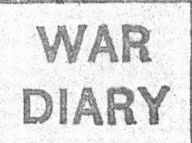

WAR DIARY

1st K. O. Y. L. I.

F E B R U A R Y

1 9 1 5

Instructions regarding War Diaries and Intelligence Summaries are contained in F. S. Regs., Part II. and the Staff Manual respectively. Title pages will be prepared in manuscript.

WAR DIARY
or
INTELLIGENCE SUMMARY
(Erase heading not required.)

Army Form C. 2118.

Hour, Date, Place	Summary of Events and Information	Remarks and references to Appendices
Feb 1st 1p.m. OULTERSTEENE	The Battalion marched to METEREN & the 83rd Bde being loaded in motor busses proceeded to VLAMMERTINGHE arriving at 6p.m after considerable delay. After a halt for food the Battalion marched towards YPRES to take over trenches from the French.	
11.30p.m	The Bn halted at the junction of the Railway & the YPRES MESSINES road to take over french stores	HKH
Feb 2nd 2a.m.	This was completed & the companies were led to their trenches by french guides.	
YPRES - COMINES	The trenches taken over by the Battalion lay on each side of the ~~LA BASSE~~ canal about 4000 yds S.E. of YPRES	
	A & B Coys occupied fire trenches S. of the Canal for about 450 yards as per attached sketch, B Coy being responsible for the canal.	HKH
	On the north side C Coy were in supporting dug-outs on the canal bank, D Coy holding the fire trenches. The machine guns were placed as per attached sketch	
6.15a.m.	The reliefs were completed. Telephone communication was at once obtained with Brigade Hd Qrs & A Coy. With B Coy there was no wire in use & N of the canal no communication could be got with C & D Coys through LA FERME CHAPELLE the senior majors post.	

1247 W 3299 200,000 (E) 8/14 J.B.C. & A. Forms/C. 2118/11.

Instructions regarding War Diaries and Intelligence Summaries are contained in F. S. Regs., Part II. and the Staff Manual respectively. Title pages will be prepared in manuscript.

WAR DIARY
or
INTELLIGENCE SUMMARY
(Erase heading not required.)

Army Form C. 2118.

Hour, Date, Place	Summary of Events and Information	Remarks and references to Appendices
11a.m – 11.30am	D Coy was subjected to somewhat heavy shell fire	
3p.m – 4 p.m.	D Coy was again subjected to heavy shell fire & suffered about 30 casualties.	HHH.
5.30 p.m.	The C.O. went over to the N. side of the canal to ascertain what was going on as no news could be got from C & D Coys. [He visited Major Gowers at LA FERME CHAPELLE & C & D Coys at their posts] returning to Bn. Hd Qrs after arranging that C Coy should relieve D Coy.	
6.25p.m.	O.C. A Coy reported a fairly heavy attack seemed to be probable but the heavy rifle fire subsided at 7.30p.m. & the night passed without further incident.	
Feb 2nd	Nothing of note occurred during the day.	5 / ...
8p.m.	The 2/Kings Own Regt commenced to relieve A Coy & the 2/E. Yorkshire Regt B & C Coys, these reliefs were completed by 4.30am & Coys	HHH
Feb 3rd	returned to billets @ LARRHOF & ROSENTHAL CHATEAUX.	HHH.
5p.m.	The battalion was ordered to move out at dusk to retake a trench taken by the Germans during the day & also to clear the woods on the N. side of the canal which were supposed to be occupied by the enemy who had broken the line.	

1247 W 3299 200,000 (E) 8/14 J.B.C.&A. Forms/C. 2118/11.

Instructions regarding War Diaries and Intelligence Summaries are contained in F. S. Regs., Part II. and the Staff Manual respectively. Title pages will be prepared in manuscript.

WAR DIARY
or
INTELLIGENCE SUMMARY.
(Erase heading not required.)

Army Form C. 2118. 5

Hour, Date, Place	Summary of Events and Information	Remarks and references to Appendices
	The trench captured by the enemy was reported to be about the left centre of the Sector N. of the canal.	
5 p.m.	The Bn moved off up the N. bank of the canal & deploying with A & B Coys in front searched the woods, which were found unoccupied by the enemy.	
10 p.m.	The Bn being reformed & supported by 3 platoons of the 2/Kings Own Regt an advance was made to the trenches in the centre of the N. Sector & the trenches, which were found to be but thinly held, seized. The Bn came under heavy shell fire during its advance & suffered some casualties. From this point it was intended to make the attack but the captured trench could not be located nor could any definite information as to its whereabouts be ascertained. The C.O. detached B Coy to attack the German trenches in front of the extreme left of the Sector in touch with the 84th Bde & withdrew the remaining 3 Coys, replacing them with 3 Platoons of the 2/Kings Own Regt. B Coy were unable to attack owing to the very intricate nature of the ground & being left in the trenches gallantly held this portion of the line for 24 hours without rations & water	51st

(73989) W4141—463. 400,000. 9/14. H.&J.Ltd. Forms/C. 2118/10.

Instructions regarding War Diaries and Intelligence Summaries are contained in F. S. Regs., Part II. and the Staff Manual respectively. Title pages will be prepared in manuscript.

WAR DIARY
or
INTELLIGENCE SUMMARY.
(Erase heading not required.)

Army Form C. 2118. 6

Hour, Date, Place	Summary of Events and Information	Remarks and references to Appendices
	The G.O.C. decided to fill up the line from the Canal to the right of the 84th Brigade as follows: C Coy was posted on the wooded hill N. of the canal to reinforce the 2/E. Yorkshire Regt & D Coy placed in the supporting dugouts. A. Coy returning to billets in reserve.	
Feb 4th 6.15 p.m.	A Coy moved out again together with the 2/E. Yorkshire Regt to again locate & attack the lost trench. Two lines of the 2/East Yorkshire Regt supported by A Coy in the 3rd line crossed our trenches with their left on the extreme left of the N. Sector & advanced some 400 yards to the S.E. Again the trench could not be located nor were any of the enemy located. The troops were then withdrawn.	HWH.
Feb 5th 6.15 p.m.	The battalion marched from the reserve Bde billets to take up quarters in the farm houses near OUDERDOM.	

SWK

Instructions regarding War Diaries and Intelligence Summaries are contained in F. S. Regs., Part II. and the Staff Manual respectively. Title pages will be prepared in manuscript.

WAR DIARY
or
INTELLIGENCE SUMMARY.
(Erase heading not required.)

Army Form C. 2118.

Hour, Date, Place	Summary of Events and Information	Remarks and references to Appendices
Feb 8th	Brig Gen. R.C. Boyle acknowledged the good work done by the Bn & thanks Lt Col C.R. Ingham Brooke for clearing up a difficult situation on the night of Feb 3rd–4th	
	The Casualties during the week ending 7th Feb were as follows: Wounded 4 officers [Capt H. Tomlinson & Capt G.H. Stanley, Lieuts H. Brysson & J.A.S. Tryhill the latter severely]	1HH
	Other Ranks Killed 11 Wounded 66 Missing 1 (believed killed) (afterwards found to be in hospital wounded)	"Trench feet" 24
OUDERDOM 11.2.15 5pm	The 83rd Brigade marched to relieve the 84th Brigade in the trenches. The trenches to be taken over were a continuation of the previous sector held by the 83rd Bde & were situated as per attached sketch. The Battalion relieved the 2nd Bn Cheshire Regt who were holding the right of the sector. The 2nd E Yorkshire Regt relieved the left of the sector, D Coy of the 1st K.O.Y.L.I. holding the two trenches N of the railway	(2)

(73989) W4141—463. 400,000. 9/14. H.&J.Ltd. Forms/C. 2118/10.

Instructions regarding War Diaries and Intelligence Summaries are contained in F. S. Regs., Part II. and the Staff Manual respectively. Title pages will be prepared in manuscript.

WAR DIARY
or
INTELLIGENCE SUMMARY.
(Erase heading not required.)

Army Form C. 2118.

8

Hour, Date, Place	Summary of Events and Information	Remarks and references to Appendices
	were under the command of the O.C. 2/E. Yorkshire Regt	
	The 1st Yorks Lancaster Regt were in support of the battalion & the 2/Kings Own in support of the left.	
10.30 p.m.	[The battalion commenced the relief]	
12.2.15 1 a.m.	The relief was reported completed	
11.55 a.m.	Head Qrs 83rd Bde reported that the left of the 83rd Bde immediately on our right was being heavily attacked. On reports being called for & a personal reconnaissance by the C.O. this was found to be incorrect & was duly reported to Hd Qrs 83rd Brigade.	
3 p.m.–4 p.m.	Our artillery shelled enemys Machine Gun on Hill 60	
3.45 p.m.	Battalion H.Qrs shelled	
7 p.m.	C.O. visited trenches held by B and C Coys (Shelled)	
13.2.15 8 a.m.	Battalion H.Qrs shelled	

9

Instructions regarding War Diaries and Intelligence Summaries are contained in F. S. Regs., Part II. and the Staff Manual respectively. Title pages will be prepared in manuscript.

WAR DIARY
or
INTELLIGENCE SUMMARY.
(*Erase heading not required.*)

Army Form C. 2118.

Hour, Date, Place	Summary of Events and Information	Remarks and references to Appendices
10.35 a.m.	Trenches occupied by B Coy shelled 2 casualties	
12.20 p.m.	Support shelter trenches N of the Railway shelled	
9.30 p.m.	Relief by 1st Yorks & Lancaster Regt commenced	HKH
14.2.15 2.30 a.m.	Relief reported completed. A & B Coys went in to the support trenches (Shelter) C & D Coys and Bn Hd Qrs returning to the Infantry Barracks at YPRES	HKH.
11.2.15 to 15.2.15	Casualties 2 killed 15 wounded	
YPRES 15.2.15 9.30 p.m.	The Battalion commenced the relief of the 1st Yorks Lancaster Regt The companies occupying the same positions as before	HKH
16.2.15 12.45 a.m.	The relief was completed	
8.15 am	Battalion Headquarters shelled	HKH

5100

Instructions regarding War Diaries and Intelligence Summaries are contained in F. S. Regs., Part II. and the Staff Manual respectively. Title pages will be prepared in manuscript.

WAR DIARY
or
INTELLIGENCE SUMMARY.
(*Erase heading not required.*)

Army Form C. 2118.

10

Hour, Date, Place	Summary of Events and Information	Remarks and references to Appendices
	All companies reported the trenches had fallen in considerably owing to the wet weather & asked for plenty of sandbags.	
9 p.m.	[The trenches occupied by C Coy (Fusiliers 2) reported to be attacked. Report found to be incorrect.] Heavy firing was opened by the enemy all along our front in which our troops did not participate	
9.25 p.m	All quiet	
17.2.15 2.45 a.m.	Heavy [illegible] gun & rifle fire on our right but no news of any attack	
3.5 a.m	O.C. A Coy reported all quiet & no attack so far as he could ascertain	
6.45 a.m	83rd Brigade reported that 2 trenches [illegible] of the railway held by 2nd E. Yorkshire Regt. blown in & attacked [illegible]. O.C. B Coy was ordered to give all assistance possible.	
12.15 p.m	O.C. No 10 Platoon opened rapid fire on 100 Germans retiring down the railway line. Afterwards the trench was heavily shelled	
12.30 p.m. to 1.30 p.m	Heavy shelling by both sides [illegible] of the [illegible].	
1.25 p.m	O.C. A Coy reported that the [illegible] on his right expected attack. Message sent to [illegible] officer	

57 [illegible]

Instructions regarding War Diaries and Intelligence Summaries are contained in F. S. Regs., Part II. and the Staff Manual respectively. Title pages will be prepared in manuscript.

WAR DIARY

or

INTELLIGENCE SUMMARY.

(*Erase heading not required.*)

Army Form C. 2118.

Hour, Date, Place	Summary of Events and Information	Remarks and references to Appendices
2.45 p.m.	Message received through O.C. A Coy that the Welsh Regt had been obliged to leave a portion of their trench owing to enfilade fire.	
3.15 p.m.	O.C. C Coy reported small parties of the enemy crossing railway line & apparently concentrating on Hill 60.	
3.30 p.m.	Half a Coy 1st York & Lancaster Regt ordered up to support C Coy & half a Coy to support A Coy.	
4 p.m.	Two of the above platoons moved to support C Coy & one platoon to support A Coy.	
9 p.m.	1st York & Lancaster Rgt commenced relieving the battalion	
18.2.15 12.50 a.m.	Relief completed. Half A Coy remaining in support of the [illegible] with one Machine Gun. B & C Coys going to support [illegible] @ [illegible]. ½ A Coy, D Coy & Headquarters returning to Infantry Barracks at YPRES.	51/c
17th	[The attached messages A1 & A2 received.]	

(73989) W4141—463. 400,000. 9/14. H.&J.Ltd. Forms/C. 2118/10.

Instructions regarding War Diaries and Intelligence Summaries are contained in F. S. Regs., Part II. and the Staff Manual respectively. Title pages will be prepared in manuscript.

WAR DIARY
or
INTELLIGENCE SUMMARY.
(Erase heading not required.)

Army Form C. 2118.

Hour, Date, Place	Summary of Events and Information	Remarks and references to Appendices
19.2.15	The Battalion took over the left section N.E. of the railway as per attached sketch. (3) Three coys 4th Yorks Regt, One Coy of Kings Own & one coy 1st York & Lancaster Regt also being in this section. Commander left section Lt Col C R Ingham Brooke.	
9.30 p.m.	Relief commenced from O.C. 2/Kings Own Regt.	
20.2.15 3.30 a.m.	Relief completed	
	Quiet all day slight shelling near support trenches & Battalion Headquarters about 8 p.m.	
8 p.m.	Battalion relieved by 13th Brigade ([illegible]) West Riding Regt	
21.2.15 12.30 a.m.	Relief completed & coys returned independently to YPRES & thence to billets at [illegible]	
	Casualties 5 killed 24 wounded 2 died of wounds "Trench Feet" 78.	
	Weather dull & mild	

(73989) W4141—463. 400,000. 9/14. H.&J.Ltd. Forms/C. 2118/10.

Instructions regarding War Diaries and Intelligence Summaries are contained in F. S. Regs., Part II. and the Staff Manual respectively. Title pages will be prepared in manuscript.

WAR DIARY
or
INTELLIGENCE SUMMARY
(Erase heading not required.)

Army Form C. 2118.

13.

Hour, Date, Place	Summary of Events and Information	Remarks and references to Appendices
OUDERDOM 26.2.15 5p.m.	The Battalion marched out to relief trench arriving at YPRES 6.45 p.m where tea was served.	
9.30 p.m	Headquarters, 2 Machine guns & A Coy relieved the Headquarters & one company of the 2nd Bn K.O.Y.L.I at BLAVERPORT. B Coy relieved 1 Coy K.O.Y.L.I in P3 (Sketch 2). Relief completed at 11.30 p.m. C Coy remained in Support in the Area D 3 Platoons in TUILLERIES (sketch 3) & 1 platoon in A2 (sketch 3). D Coy relieved fire trench 40 (sketch 3). These 2 Coys are under command of Area D Commander. Nothing unusual occurred.	HHH
28.2.15	Headquarters took over from 1st York & Lancaster at VERBRANDENMOLEN. A Coy occupying trenches 33 & 34 (sketch 2) B Coy trench 35. One Coy 1st York & Lancaster Regt held 36 & 37. C & D Coys remained as before.	HHH
1.3.15 8.55 a.m	Enemy threw a bomb into 35 killing 1 & wounding 5. Successful retaliation was made & no reply received.	
4.30 p.m to 5 p.m	35, 36 & 37 shelled but no damage done.	

1247 W 3299 200,000 (E) 8/14 J.B.C. & A. Forms/C. 2118/11.

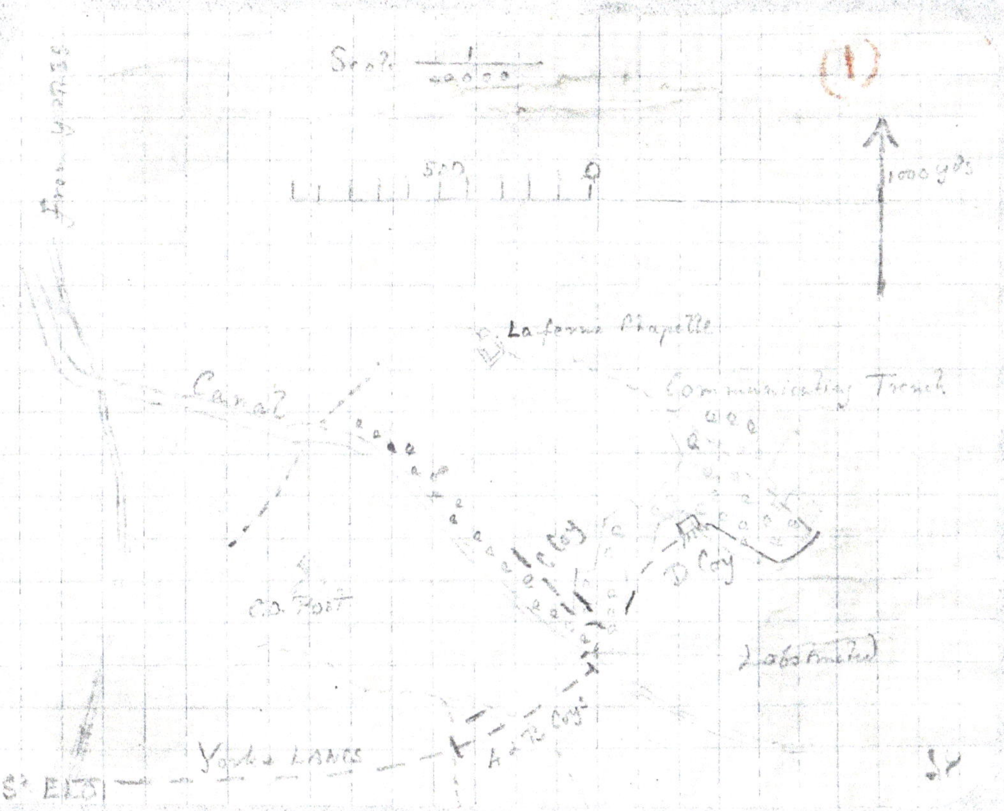
(1)
500
0
1000 yds
La ferme Chapelle
Canal
Communicating Trench
C Coy
D Coy
A & B Coys
Yorks & Lancs

(3)

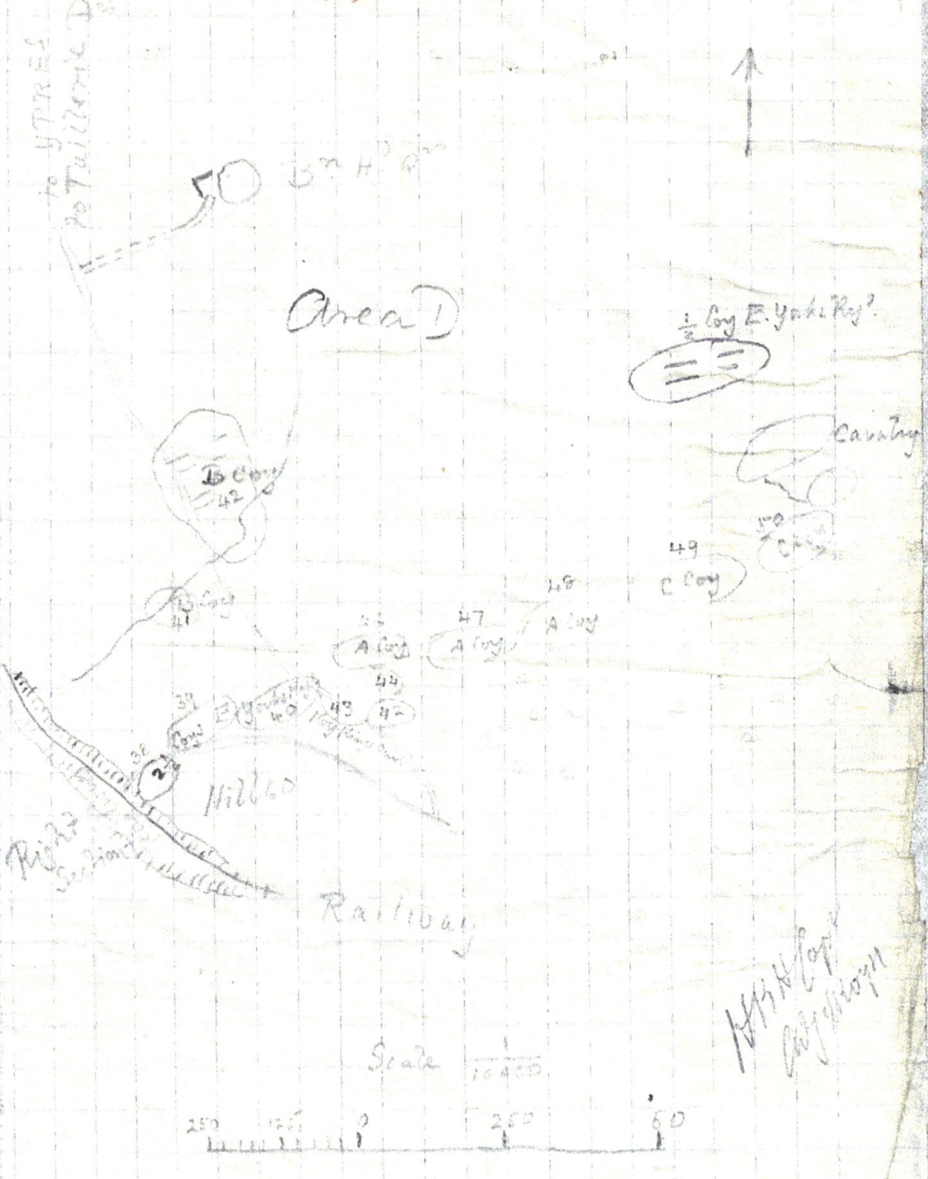
to YPRES
Area D
½ Coy E. Yorks Regt
Cavalry
49
C Coy
48
A Coy
47
A Coy
A Coy
44
43
42
B Coy
42
41
Hill 60
Railway
Scale 1/10,000
250
0
250
500

"A" Form. Army Form

MESSAGES AND SIGNALS.

No. of Message

...m. ...ictions.	Words 41	Charge	This message is on a/c of:	Recd. at
C	Sent At ... m. To By		... Service. (Signature of "Franking Officer.")	Date From By

TO	O	C	ALL	UNITS
	83rd	Brigade	(A1)	

* Sender's Number	Day of Month	In reply to Number	AAA
BM 265	17th		

message recieved from commander fifth corps begins very glad to hear your message BM 262 I am sure you and your brigade have done very good work today ends

From
Place 83rd BDE
Time 9.43 PM

The above may be forwarded as now correct...

(Z)

Signature of Addressor or person authorised to telegraph in his name

* This ... erased if not required.

"A" Form. Army Form C. 2121

MESSAGES AND SIGNALS.

No. of Message

Prefix SH Code 11RP m. Office of Origin and Service Instructions.	Words 24	Charge	This message is on a/c of: Service. (Signature of "Franking Officer.")	Recd. at m.
2 HC	Sent			Date
	At m.			From
	To			
	By			By

TO	O	C	HOYL
	(A2)	YL	

Sender's Number	Day of Month	In reply to Number	AAA
KA266	Seventeenth		

message received from G O C Twenty eighth Division begins congratulations on excellent work result as I always expected Bulfin ends

From	83 RD	BDE
Place		
Time	9.43 PM	

The above may be forwarded as now corrected. (Z)

Censor. Signature of Addressor or person authorised to telegraph in his

* This line should be erased if not required.

... Ltd. W... W5673/619—50,000. 10/14. Forms C2121/10.

Scale $\frac{1}{10000}$.

(2.)

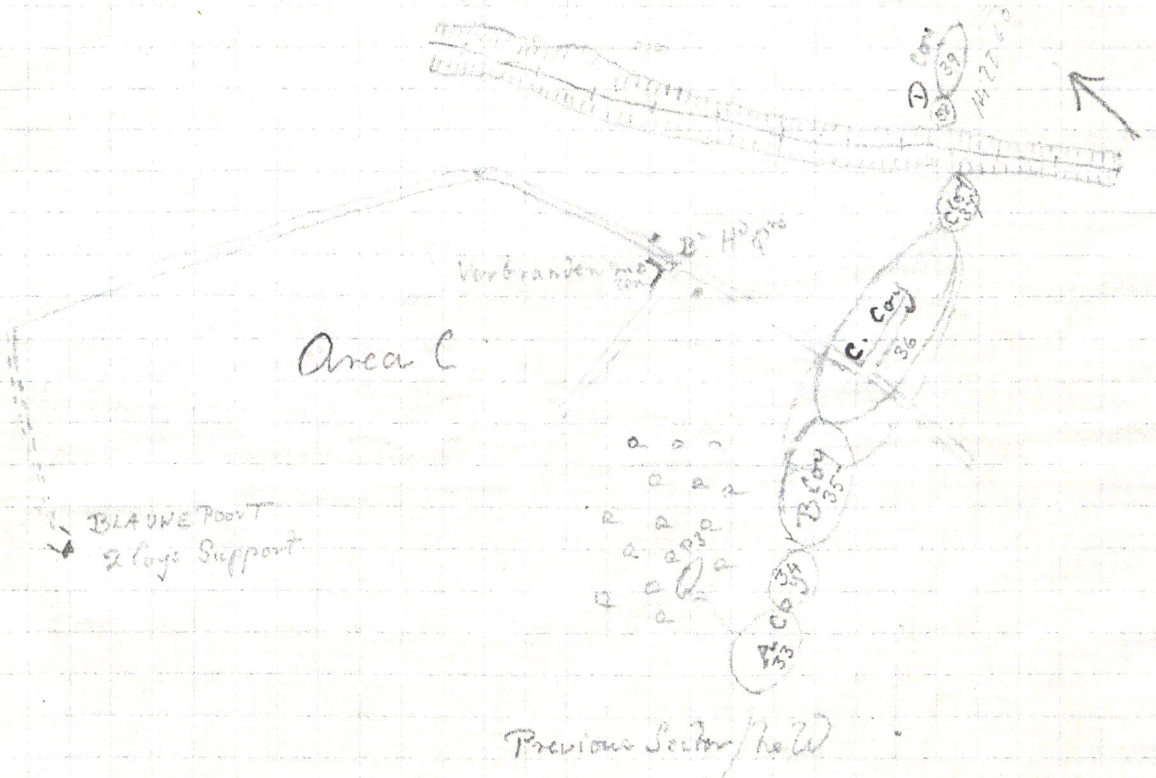

83rd Bde.
28th Div.

WAR
DIARY

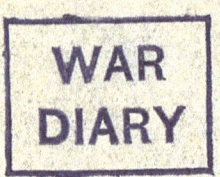

Attached with Bde. to 5th Div. from 3rd March.

1st K. O. Y. L. I.

M A R C H

1 9 1 5

14.

Instructions regarding War Diaries and Intelligence Summaries are contained in F. S. Regs., Part II. and the Staff Manual respectively. Title pages will be prepared in manuscript.

WAR DIARY
or
INTELLIGENCE SUMMARY
(Erase heading not required.)

Army Form C. 2118.

1st K.O.Y.L.I. March 1915

Hour, Date, Place	Summary of Events and Information	Remarks and references to Appendices
March 1st. 9 p.m.	The A & B Coys were relieved by 2nd Bn K.O.Y.L.I. Relief completed 10.30 p.m. C & D Coys were relieved by the K.O.S.B.	
2.3.15 1.30 am	The Battalion was billeted in VLAMERTINGHE	HKH
3.3.15 8 a.m.	The Battalion marched to billets at BAILLEUL forming part of the 5th Division of 2nd Army. Weather during this period was dull & cold. Casualties 1 killed 1 died of wounds 13 wounded	HKH.
7.3.15 BAILLEUL	The Battalion marched out and went into Support of Sector D (see sketch 4) at LINDENHOEK relieving 2/Cheshire Regt.	HKH.
11.3.15	The Battalion took over the trenches in SECTOR D from 1st York & Lancaster Regt. Relief completed at 11.30 p.m. Four platoons of 5th Kings Own were attached to the Regt one to each Coy. The Battalion was disposed of as under (see sketch 4)	HKH.

Trenches					
14A, 13, 13AS	A. Coy	11b, 11a, 11aS, No 5 Support	D Coy	R.E. FARM	B. Coy
12, 12S	C Coy			Dressing Station	1 Sect. C Coy & M.O.
				ELBOW FARM	Bn. HdQrs

03

Instructions regarding War Diaries and Intelligence Summaries are contained in F. S. Regs., Part II. and the Staff Manual respectively. Title pages will be prepared in manuscript.

WAR DIARY
or
INTELLIGENCE SUMMARY
(Erase heading not required.)

Army Form C. 2118.

15

Hour, Date, Place	Summary of Events and Information	Remarks and references to Appendices
	The Company are R.E. Farm was placed under the orders of the O.C. 59th Coy R.E. & ordered to BURNT FARM	
12.3.15 12.15 a.m.	The Commanding Officer transferred his Headquarters to R.E. Farm on account of the impending attack by the 3rd Division on HILL 76.	HKH.
12.40 a.m	The Commanding Officer visited trenches 14A, 13, 13S and supporting Point No5 returning to R.E. FARM at 2.15 a.m. which the Headquarters of the 24th Brigade ~~had~~ ~~[illegible]~~ HKH occupied	
7 a.m.	The 3rd Division was entrusted with the attack on HILL 76 which was timed to start with the artillery bombardment at 7 a.m. The battalion being ordered to open heavy fire at 8.30 a.m. Owing to the ~~[illegible]~~ HKH day being very misty & dull the attack was postponed.	
2 p.m.	The mist began to clear	
3.30 p.m.	The attack commenced by heavy gun fire on enemy position	
3.40 p.m.	Orders were received for the battalion to open heavy fire at 4 p.m.	
3.45 p.m.	Lull in artillery fire	

1247 W 3299 200,000 (E) 8/14 J.B.C. & A. Forms/C. 2118/11.

Instructions regarding War Diaries and Intelligence Summaries are contained in F. S. Regs., Part II. and the Staff Manual respectively. Title pages will be prepared in manuscript.

WAR DIARY
or
INTELLIGENCE SUMMARY

(Erase heading not required.)

Army Form C. 2118.

16

Hour, Date, Place	Summary of Events and Information	Remarks and references to Appendices
3.50 p.m.	Final bombardment commenced	
3.59 p.m.	Heavy rifle and machine gun fire opened	
4.10 p.m.	3rd Division timed to commence attack	
4.20 p.m.	R.E. FARM shelled	
4.40 p.m.	Fire died down somewhat, sharp bursts of rifle fire breaking out at intervals	
6.10 p.m.	Fire quieted down	
6.20 p.m.	Fired died away	
	Casualties during the action 2 Officers wounded (1 died of wounds) other ranks 6 killed 17 wounded. Two machine Guns disabled	2/Lt Thorpe died of wounds 2/Lt Hutchinson slightly wounded
~~10.0 p.m.~~ 10 p.m.	Commanding Officer visited trenches 12, 12S 11b 11a & 11as returning to original Headquarters at ELBOW FARM at midnight.	51
13.3.15 5 a.m.	Company at BURNT FARM moved to R.E. FARM handing over to 3rd Monmouthshire Regt. ceasing to be under the command of the O.C. 59 Coy R.E.	
6 p.m.	Situation quiet some shelling during the afternoon. Heavy gun fire could be heard from the North about St. ELOI	

Instructions regarding War Diaries and Intelligence Summaries are contained in F. S. Regs., Part II. and the Staff Manual respectively. Title pages will be prepared in manuscript.

WAR DIARY
or
INTELLIGENCE SUMMARY
(Erase heading not required.)

Army Form C. 2118. 17

Hour, Date, Place		Summary of Events and Information	Remarks and references to Appendices
14.3.15	6 p.m.	Enemy showed more activity in rifle fire during the day	
	6.45 p.m.	Message received from 83rd Bde that reliefs would not be proceeded with till the situation was cleared up, referring presumably to the heavy firing in the direction of ST ELOI.	
	9.30 p.m.	Reliefs cancelled	
15.3.15	4.50 a.m.	Heavy firing from the direction of St ELOI	
	7 a.m.	Situation normal	
	7 p.m.	The Commanding officer visited all trenches	
16.3.15		Situation abnormally quiet. Weather dull and misty	
	8 p.m.	C.O visited DRESSING STATION & R.E. FARM. Senior Major visited all trenches.	51
17.3.15		Situation very quiet. Weather dull & misty.	
	7.45 p.m.	1st Yorks Lancaster Regt took over Bn HdQrs at ELBOW FARM	
	10 p.m.	All reliefs were completed. 1st Yorks Lancaster Regt transferred their HdQrs to R.E FARM. The battalion returned to billets in LINDENHOEK.	
19.3.15	3 p.m.	The battalion marched back to St JANS CAPELLE & went into billets.	

1247 W 3299 200,000 (E) 8/14 J.B.C. & A. Forms/C. 2118/11.

Instructions regarding War Diaries and Intelligence Summaries are contained in F. S. Regs., Part II. and the Staff Manual respectively. Title pages will be prepared in manuscript.

WAR DIARY
or
INTELLIGENCE SUMMARY

(Erase heading not required.)

Army Form C. 2118.

Hour, Date, Place	Summary of Events and Information	Remarks and references to Appendices
23·3·15 5 p.m.	The Battalion marched out and relieved the 1st York & Lancaster Regt in trenches 14B to 11B inclusive. The Battalion also took over R.E. FARM as Regtl HdQrs COB Farm & ~~Tea~~ farm (Sketch)	HKH
11·30 pm	Reliefs completed	
24·3·15 6 a.m.	Situation quiet. Magnetic N. from trench 13 a communication trench was reported to run about 600x back to a second line of fire trenches. This trench had dugouts on each side. This was pointed out to the O.C. 80th Bat. R.F.A.	HKH
25·3·15 ~~10 p.m.~~ 1·30 am to 5 a.m	Enemy's trench mortars very active on our left front, but with little or no result. Otherwise situation quiet	
9·20 p.m.	Heavy rifle fire heard from the direction of St ELOI	HKH
26·3·15 8·20 am	Enemy's heavy guns dropped about $\frac{1}{2}$ a dozen shells close to R.E. Farm. Probably directed at new Dugouts & communication trenches.	HKH
11·30 am.	NEUVE EGLISE shelled	
11·45 am	Enemy's observation ~~[illegible]~~ Balloon seen over MESSINES	

1247 W 3299 200,000 (E) 8/14 J.B.C. & A. Forms/C. 2118/11.

Instructions regarding War Diaries and Intelligence Summaries are contained in F. S. Regs., Part II. and the Staff Manual respectively. Title pages will be prepared in manuscript.

WAR DIARY
or
INTELLIGENCE SUMMARY
(Erase heading not required.)

Army Form C. 2118.

19

Hour, Date, Place		Summary of Events and Information	Remarks and references to Appendices
	10.10 a.m.	"80" Battery R.F.A. registered on German communication trench reported on 23rd inst. Eighteen shells were fired the last two dropping into the trench.	
	2.45 p.m.	Enemys big guns fired H.E. shells on the W. side of R.E. Farm from an angle of 92°	
	6 p.m.	Situation normal.	
27.3.15	6 am.	Enemys aeroplane crossed our lines at 4.50 am. Situation quiet.	
28.3.15	1.30 p.m	Enemy shelled WULVERGEM with H.E.	
	6 p.m	Situation quiet	
29.3.15	6 a.m.	Situation quiet. Enemys transport believed to have been heard in MESSINES about 11.45 p.m (28.3.15)	
	9.30 p.m	Battalion relieved by 1st York & Lancaster Regt & returned to billets at ALDERSHOT CAMP West of NEUVE EGLISE	
		Casualties during the tour 1 man killed 8 wounded 1 " died of wounds 1 officer wounded (Lieut Thwaytes)	

Army Form C. 2118.

WAR DIARY
or
INTELLIGENCE SUMMARY.
(Erase heading not required.)

Instructions regarding War Diaries and Intelligence Summaries are contained in F. S. Regs., Part II. and the Staff Manual respectively. Title pages will be prepared in manuscript.

Place	Date	Hour	Summary of Events and Information	Remarks and references to Appendices

D. D. & L., London, E.C.
(10304) Wt W5300/P713 750,000 3/18 E 2688 Forms C/2118/14.

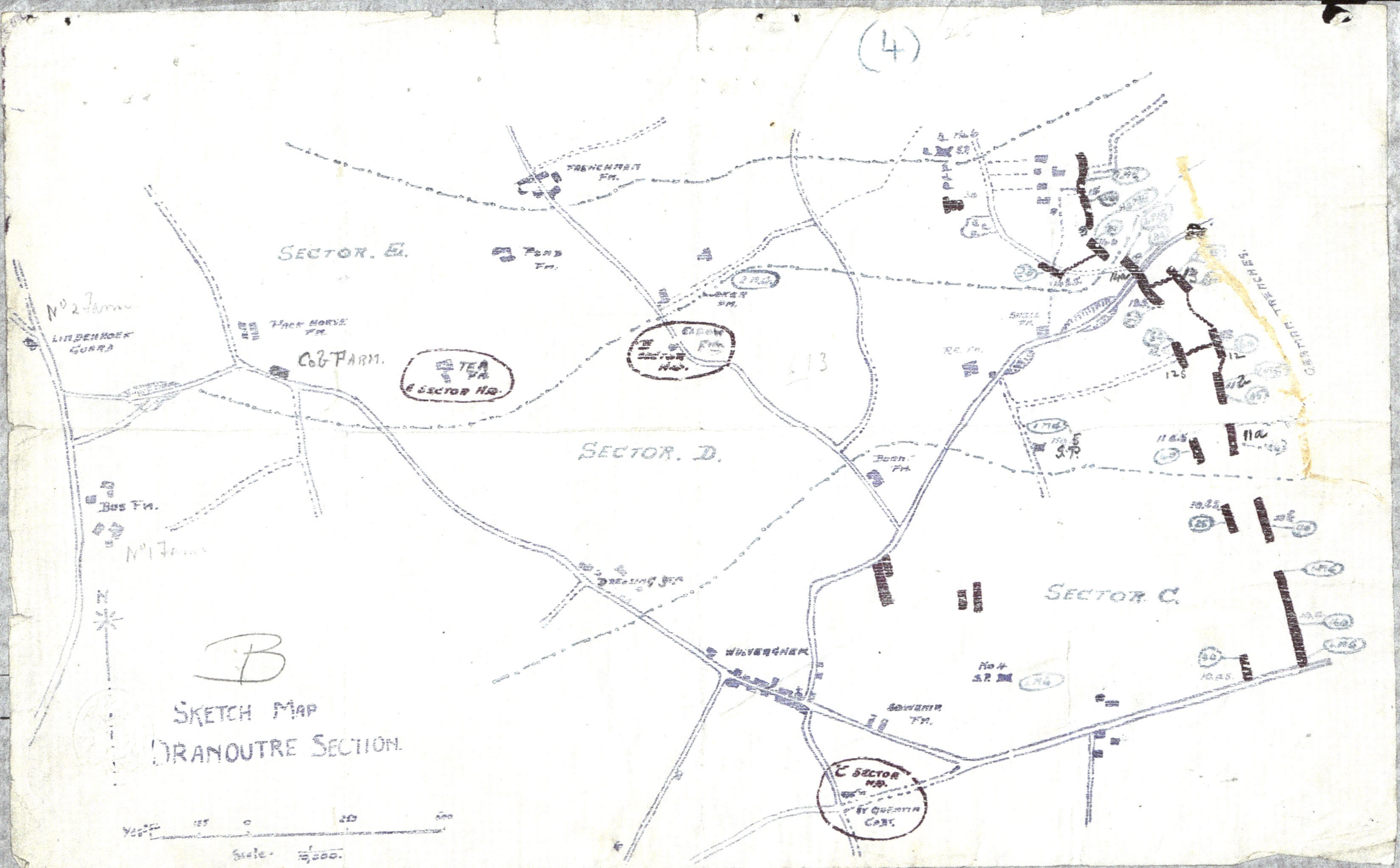
(4)
SKETCH MAP
DRANOUTRE SECTION.
B
Scale 1/10,000.
SECTOR. E.
SECTOR. D.
SECTOR. C.
No 2 Farm
LINDENHOEK GUARD
No 1 Farm
Bos Fm.
Pack Horse Fm.
C&G FARM.
TEA FM.
E SECTOR HQ.
Pond Fm.
Frenchman Fm.
Elbow Fm.
D Sector HQ.
Locker Fm.
Dressing Stn
Wulverghem
Sonnen Fm.
Boer Fm.
R.E. Fm.
Shell Fm.
No 5 S.P.
No 4 S.P.
C SECTOR HQ.
St Quentin Cabt.
GERMAN TRENCHES.
13
12
12S
11a
11a
N

83rd Bde.
28th Div.

WAR
DIARY

Returned with Bde. from 5th Div. 6.4.15.

1st K. O. Y. L. I.

A P R I L

1 9 1 5

83/78

1/KOYLI

1-30 April

1915

Instructions regarding War Diaries and Intelligence Summaries are contained in F. S. Regs., Part II. and the Staff Manual respectively. Title pages will be prepared in manuscript.

WAR DIARY
or
INTELLIGENCE SUMMARY
(Erase heading not required.)

Army Form C. 2118. 18

Hour, Date, Place	Summary of Events and Information	Remarks and references to Appendices
2·4·15 Aldershot Camp 2·15p.m. Neuve Eglise	The battalion marched into billets at BOESCHEPE via BAILLEUL	
BOESCHEPE ·7·4·15 11a.m.	The brigade was inspected by the Army Commander, General Smith-Dorien. The Army commander thanked the brigade for the excellent work done in the trenches by them while in the 5th Division.	HKH
	The brigade was transferred to the 28th Division	
9·4·15 YPRES	The battalion marched to YPRES & was billeted in the Lunatic Asylum	
YPRES 7p.m. 12·4·15	The battalion marched out of the MENIN GATE to relieve the 2nd Bn East Yorkshire Regt holding the Right Section of the 83rd Brigade S. of ZONNEBEKE 4 miles 760 yards N. of YPRES. see attached sketch (5)	HKH
13·4·15 1·15a.m.	Reliefs completed	
	The trench were in a very wooded country. The battalion HdQrs and the 1 Coy in support were in dugouts	HKH

Instructions regarding War Diaries and Intelligence Summaries are contained in F. S. Regs., Part II. and the Staff Manual respectively. Title pages will be prepared in manuscript.

WAR DIARY
or
INTELLIGENCE SUMMARY
(Erase heading not required.)

Army Form C. 2118.

Hour, Date, Place	Summary of Events and Information	Remarks and references to Appendices
	A trench was in indifferent repair as to the parapets and traverses were lacking. This trench was enfiladed from the right. The Germans had sapped to within a few yards of the houses. The fire trench B was also in very bad repair as to drainage & parapets. There were no traverses and the men occupied "bays" in the trench. This trench was enfiladed from the right. This trench could not be reached by day as the enemy could fire straight down the communication trench. The support trench of B was in good repair. C trench was also in good repair	
13.4.15 9 a.m.	The Machine Gun officer Lieut. A. C. Collis-Browne was shot through the head in A trench & died a few hours afterwards. The day passed quietly but the enemy did considerable damage to C trench parapets with a kind of small trench gun	
14.4.15	The day again passed quietly. Enemy's trench gun was still a nuisance	

1247 W 3299 200,000 (E) 8/14 J.B.C. & A. Forms/C. 2118/11.

Instructions regarding War Diaries and Intelligence Summaries are contained in F. S. Regs., Part II. and the Staff Manual respectively. Title pages will be prepared in manuscript.

WAR DIARY
or
INTELLIGENCE SUMMARY
(Erase heading not required.)

Army Form C. 2118.

Hour, Date, Place	Summary of Events and Information	Remarks and references to Appendices
15 5.15 p.m.	Enemy massed some guns on a party 5th King's Own working close to Bn HdQrs. Putting some 15 shells into them inside a minute causing considerable casualties.	
15.4.15	Day passed quietly, it was found the trench guns soon stopped if the offending trench received a few rounds of shrapnel.	
8 p.m.	The ~~following~~ attached message (6) was received and acted upon.	
16.4.15 1 p.m.	2nd East Yorkshire Regt arrived at Bn HdQrs.	
3.15 p.m.	Relief was completed & the Battalion returned to POPITJE just above a mile E of YPRES. At 7a.m. as all remained quiet the battalion received orders to return to the Huts about 1 mile W. of YPRES arriving there 8.30a.m.	
	Weather during this period was on the whole fine & bright. Except the morning of 14th.	
	Casualties 1 Officer killed, 4 other ranks killed. 1 Officer Wounded (Lt Houghton), 12 other ranks killed	

1247 W 3299 200,000 (E) 8/14 J.B.C. & A. Forms/C. 2118/11.

Instructions regarding War Diaries and Intelligence Summaries are contained in F. S. Regs., Part II. and the Staff Manual respectively. Title pages will be prepared in manuscript.

WAR DIARY
or
INTELLIGENCE SUMMARY
(Erase heading not required.)

Army Form C. 2118.

Hour, Date, Place	Summary of Events and Information	Remarks and references to Appendices
Huts between YPRES and VLAMERTINGHE 7p.m 19th 4.15	The battalion marched out & took over A, B & C Trenches, now renamed No1, No2 & No3 respectively, from 2nd East Yorkshire Regt	
11.45p.m	Relief completed	
8a.m. 20.4.15	The right detached portion of No1 Trench was heavily shelled by H.E. shells and knocked to pieces. 2/Lt A.M.E. Scrabey 3rd Somerset Light Infantry, the platoon Sgt & eight men were killed and ten men wounded.	
9a.m.	2/Lt Boone visited the detached trench. He found 12 men still holding the post	
4.30p.m	2/Lt Boone W.C. who remained in command of the detached trench was killed.	
21.4.14	The situation continued normal. Lt Hine-Haycock was wounded about 5.30p.m. on 21st & 2/Lt Munroe was wounded about 4a.m 22nd.	
22nd 4.15 6.30p.m	Heavy artillery fire broke out to the N. & continued till 7.30pm. The Canadian division report an attack on trenches on their left presumably N. of ZONNEBEKE.	
23.4.15 9.30am	Enemy reported to have attacked the French on the left of the Canadian division, preceding the attack with asphixiating gas.	

Instructions regarding War Diaries and Intelligence Summaries are contained in F. S. Regs., Part II. and the Staff Manual respectively. Title pages will be prepared in manuscript.

WAR DIARY
or
INTELLIGENCE SUMMARY
(Erase heading not required.)

Army Form C. 2118.

Hour, Date, Place		Summary of Events and Information	Remarks and references to Appendices
		The French retired on BOESINGHE, the Canadian division left flank falling back on ST JULIAN	
	3.15p.m	The woods round Battalion H.Q. were heavily shelled	
	3.25p.m	Heavy rifle fire broke out on our left probably the 84th & 85th Brigades close to ZONNEBEKE	
24.4.15	6p.m.	Enemy were reported to be advancing from ~~the North on ZONNEBEKE~~ the direction of ZEVENKOTE and A Coy under Capt Mallinson were ordered from the battalion supports to this place to reinforce	
	10p.m	This company returned, the report being found incorrect.	
	11p.m.	The attached message (7) received.	
25.4.15		Very heavy gun fire continued all day from 6a.m to 11.30pm	
	3.45pm	Information received that the French attack had been postponed	
	7pm	Attached message (8) received	
26.4.15	12.15am – 12.30am.	Heavy burst of rifle & machine gun fire on our left probably the 84th Brigade	
	9a.m.	Enemy were reported to be advancing Southwards on ZONNEBEKE and A Coy were ordered to move to the dugouts of the reserve company of the centre battalion 83rd Brigade	

1247 W 3299 200,000 (E) 8/14 J.B.C. & A. Forms/C. 2118/11.

Army Form C. 2118.

WAR DIARY
or
INTELLIGENCE SUMMARY
(Erase heading not required.)

Instructions regarding War Diaries and Intelligence Summaries are contained in F. S. Regs., Part II. and the Staff Manual respectively. Title pages will be prepared in manuscript.

Hour, Date, Place		Summary of Events and Information	Remarks and references to Appendices
26-4-15	8.30 p.m.	A. Coy returned to Battalion H.Q. not having been moved from the reserve dugouts.	
		Draft of 40 men arrived [and joined Quarter Master who was with 2nd line transport.]	KCT KCT
27-4-15.		Battalion in trenches. Intermittent shelling.	
	11 p.m.	Draft of 40 men arrived with rations. Remained with Batt^n H.Q.	KCT KCT
		2/Lt Bateman and 19 men joined [Quartermaster with 2nd line transport	
28-4-15.		Battalion in trenches.	KCT
		2/Lt Bateman posted to D Coy and draft distributed.	KCT
		Situation normal.	
29-4-15.		Battalion in trenches.	KCT
		Captain K. R. Davies York Regt attached 1st KOYLI wounded 10.30 a.m.	KCT

1247 W 3299 200,000 (E). 8/14 J.B.C. & A. Forms/C. 2118/11.

Instructions regarding War Diaries and Intelligence Summaries are contained in F. S. Regs., Part II. and the Staff Manual respectively. Title pages will be prepared in manuscript.

WAR DIARY
or
INTELLIGENCE SUMMARY
(Erase heading not required.)

Army Form C. 2118.

Hour, Date, Place	Summary of Events and Information	Remarks and references to Appendices
30. 4. 15.	Battalion in trenches B Coy digging new line of trenches on the FRIEZENBERG Ridge.	Sct Sct
	[signature] Major Cmdg 1st KOYLI 19 - 5 - 15	
	It is regretted that the record from the 26th is so sketchy. The C.O. & Adjt as well as many other officers became casualties on the 8 May, so that the necessary notes for bringing this diary up to date have been lost. [initials]	

1247 W 3299 200,000 (E) 8/14 J.B.C. & A. Forms/C. 2118/11.

28th Division

83/78

181/5610

War Diary of the

1st KING'S OWN YORKSHIRE LIGHT INFANTRY.

from. 1-5-15. to 31-5-15.

Volume. V.

04

15 sheet

War Diary of the

1st KING'S OWN YORKSHIRE LIGHT INFANTRY.

from. 1. 5-15. to 31-5-15.

Volume. V.

Instructions regarding War Diaries and Intelligence Summaries are contained in F. S. Regs., Part II. and the Staff Manual respectively. Title pages will be prepared in manuscript.

WAR DIARY
or
~~INTELLIGENCE SUMMARY~~
(Erase heading not required.)

Army Form C. 2118.

Page 1

Hour, Date, Place	Summary of Events and Information	Remarks and references to Appendices
May 1st	Battalion in trenches A Coy digging on FRIEZENBERG line	SCS
2nd	Battalion in trenches Order received that trenches in ZONNEKE line would probably be evacuated and all trench stores, ammunition etc would be sent back to FREIZENBERG line	SCS SCS
11 pm	Order re retirement cancelled	SCS
3rd	Battalion in trenches	SCS
4 pm	Order received to retire to new position. New line occupied. 1st KOYLI returned to huts W of YPRES	SCS
4th	Battalion in huts.	SCS

Instructions regarding War Diaries and Intelligence Summaries are contained in F. S. Regs., Part II. and the Staff Manual respectively. Title pages will be prepared in manuscript.

WAR DIARY
or
~~INTELLIGENCE SUMMARY~~
(Erase heading not required.)

Army Form C. 2118.

Hour, Date, Place	Summary of Events and Information	Remarks and references to Appendices
May 5th 7.30 pm	Battalion moved into dug outs behind the [illegible] R. trenches at FRIEZENBERG.	[illegible]
6th	Battalion in dug outs.	[illegible]
7th	Battalion in dug outs.	
11 pm	Moved into fire trenches.	
8th	Trenches heavily shelled with high explosive; this was followed by a German attack. C & D Companies were shelled out of their trenches. A & B drove off the German attack and withdrew from trenches at night and went to 80th Brigade.	[illegible]
	Casualties. Killed 2 Captain [illegible], Capt K. Lambert, Lieut [illegible] Palmer [illegible] and 2Lt J.A.R. Ferguson Royal [illegible] Regt.	[illegible]

Army Form C. 2118.

Instructions regarding War Diaries and Intelligence Summaries are contained in F. S. Regs., Part II. and the Staff Manual respectively. Title pages will be prepared in manuscript.

WAR DIARY
or
~~INTELLIGENCE SUMMARY~~
(Erase heading not required.)

Hour, Date, Place	Summary of Events and Information	Remarks and references to Appendices
May 8th	Died of wounds 1 Lieut C.H. Wharton D.L.I.	
	Wounded 1 Major C.R. Ingham Burke 2 Lt Hutchison 1st KOYLI	E.S.
	and 2Lt W.W. Ousbridge E. Yorks.	
	Missing 1 2Lt W. Bateman 1st Y&L and Capt R.C.L.	E.S.
	Elvery R.A.M.C.	
	Regimental Sergeant Major Lesh was also killed	E.S.
	Casualties in other ranks, from 19-4-15 to 7-5-15	
	Killed 34 Died of wounds 3 Wounded 112	E.S.
	Casualties on 8th	
	Killed 83 Wounded 92 Missing 212	E.S.
	The four machine guns were either destroyed by shell fire or buried.	
9th	Draft of 136 men under 2Lieut C.T. Bewitt L.A.B. arrived.	E.S.
11 pm	Battalion came out of trenches to huts W of YPRES	E.S.

1247 W 3299 200,000 (E) 8/14 J.B.C. & A. Forms/C. 2118/11.

Instructions regarding War Diaries and Intelligence Summaries are contained in F. S. Regs., Part II. and the Staff Manual respectively. Title pages will be prepared in manuscript.

WAR DIARY
or
~~INTELLIGENCE SUMMARY~~
(Erase heading not required.)

Army Form C. 2118.

4

Hour, Date, Place		Summary of Events and Information	Remarks and references to Appendices
May 10th		Remainder of 83rd Bde formed into a composite Battalion under Lt Col Worsley [illegible] 3rd Monmouths	
	6.30 p.m	Lt J. A. Lewis joined Battn from 28th Divisional [illegible] Coy and took over duties of Adjutant	
	7.30 p.m	Battalion marched out of huts. Strength [illegible] officers and 400 other ranks.	
	7 pm	Capt R. E. Warden admitted to Hospital sick	
		Battalion went into dug outs W. of POTIZJE. Carrying up stores to trenches.	
11th	1.0 am	Returned 1.0 am Casualty 1 man wounded.	
	8.30 pm	Battalion [left dug outs and] went into bivouac [in BRANDHOEK – ELVERDINGHE road] in wood 2000x	
	11.15 pm	N.N.W. of Brandhoek.	
		3 2/Lieuts [R.O. Acherley SWB and 2 Lieut A.E. Keuthe and J.L. Steele KOYLI] joined	
12th	10.0 am	2Lt Robinson 1st KOYLI returned from machine gun course at St OMER.	

Instructions regarding War Diaries and Intelligence Summaries are contained in F. S. Regs., Part II. and the Staff Manual respectively. Title pages will be prepared in manuscript.

WAR DIARY

or

~~INTELLIGENCE SUMMARY~~

(Erase heading not required.)

Army Form C. 2118.

5.

Hour, Date, Place		Summary of Events and Information	Remarks and references to Appendices
May 12th	6.30 pm	Battalion moved from bivouac into billets in farm on POPERINGHE – ELVERDINGHE road about 3000x N.E of POPERINGHE.	S.C.S.
13th		Battalion remained in Billets.	S.C.S.
14th	8.30 a.m	Battalion moved from billets by motor bus into farms in the vicinity of WINNIEZEELE.	S.C.S.
		Lieut L.T. WELLS R.A.M.C. joined	S.C.S.
15th	8.30 pm	Battalion at WINNIEZEELE. Draft of 71 N.C.O's and men under command of 2/Lt A.F. Ackerman West Surrey Regiment, and 2/Lt O.F.P. Marshall R.W.K. joined	S.C.S.
16th		Battalion at WINNIEZEELE. Companies exercised in drill and musketry	S.C.S.

1247 W 3299 200,000 (E) 8/14 J.B.C. & A. Forms/C. 2118/11.

Instructions regarding War Diaries and Intelligence Summaries are contained in F. S. Regs., Part II. and the Staff Manual respectively. Title pages will be prepared in manuscript.

WAR DIARY
or
INTELLIGENCE SUMMARY
(Erase heading not required.)

Army Form C. 2118.

6.

Hour, Date, Place	Summary of Events and Information	Remarks and references to Appendices
May 17th. 9.30 am	Battalion inspected by Lt Col T. A. [illegible] Welch Regiment acting Brigadier 93rd Brigade. He expressed himself very pleased with the Transport, rifles and turn out of the men. He also inspected the billets.	[illegible]
12.30 pm	Major C. E. Beckwith D.S.O. joined from 2nd [illegible] and took over command.	[illegible]
4.30 pm	2 Lt [W. E. Roscoe] West Yorkshire Regiment joined	[illegible]
18th	Battalion exercised at drill. C.O. inspected the billets.	
1 pm	2/Lieut [O. Wilson] West Yorkshire Regiment joined	[illegible]
19th	Company parades in morning.	
2.30 pm	Sergeant major parade. 2 Lt Robinson proceeded on leave.	

1247 W 3299 200,000 (E) 8/14 J.B.C. & A. Forms/C. 2118/11.

Instructions regarding War Diaries and Intelligence Summaries are contained in F. S. Regs., Part II. and the Staff Manual respectively. Title pages will be prepared in manuscript.

WAR DIARY
or
~~INTELLIGENCE SUMMARY~~
(Erase heading not required.)

Army Form C. 2118.

7.

Hour, Date, Place		Summary of Events and Information	Remarks and references to Appendices
May 21st	11.30 a.m	The General Officer C-in-C addressed the 83rd Bde and congratulated them on their gallant fight in the 2nd Battle of YPRES.	[illegible]
	2 p.m	Battalion [left WINNIZEELE and marched by STEENVORDE and POPERINGHE into] billets west of VLAMERTINGHE.	[illegible]
	7.15 pm	Arrived in billets.	
	6.30 pm	2 Lieuts [L. J. Rodwyn and . Walters] 3rd Oxford and Bucks L.I. joined the Battalion	[illegible]
	8.15 pm	Capt Bond, 2 Lieuts Blewitt, Alderson, Wilson and Acherley, went up to reconnoitre trenches.	[illegible]
22nd	4 a.m.	The officers returned from reconnoitring the trenches.	[illegible]
	5.50 pm	Left VLAMERTINGHE at 5.50 pm and marched by MENIN Gate to trenches S.E. of YPRES in Sanctuary Wood	

1247 W 3299 200,000 (E) 8/14 J.B.C. & A. Forms/C. 2118/11.

Instructions regarding War Diaries and Intelligence Summaries are contained in F. S. Regs., Part II. and the Staff Manual respectively. Title pages will be prepared in manuscript.

WAR DIARY
or
~~INTELLIGENCE SUMMARY~~
(Erase heading not required.)

Army Form C. 2118.

81

Hour, Date, Place		Summary of Events and Information	Remarks and references to Appendices
May 22	9.45 pm	H.Q. Kings arrived at H.Q. 9th Royal Scots at 9.45 p.m.	TCT
	11.20 pm	Relief complete at 11.20 p.m and reported to 83rd Bde.	TCT
		A. C. D in firing line. B in support in trenches in the wood.	TCT
		Trenches from 2 with A and 2 with C. on right of Batt 2 5th Kings Own on left 1st Welch.	TCT
	11.30 pm	Captain Mellunsin visited trenches at 11.30 pm	TCT
23.	2.15 a.m	One platoon of B sent to reinforce C owing to length of trench held.	TCT
	3.30 a.m	C.O. visited trenches	
	5 a.m	Situation normal.	

1247 W 3299 200,000 (E) 8/14 J.B.C. & A. Forms/C. 2118/11.

Instructions regarding War Diaries and Intelligence Summaries are contained in F. S. Regs., Part II. and the Staff Manual respectively. Title pages will be prepared in manuscript.

WAR DIARY
or
~~INTELLIGENCE SUMMARY~~
(Erase heading not required.)

Army Form C. 2118.

9

Hour, Date, Place		Summary of Events and Information	Remarks and references to Appendices
May 23.	4 pm	C.O. and Adjutant visited trenches	[illegible]
	5 pm	Relief commenced	[illegible]
		A, B, C relieved by 5th D.G's.	
		D " " " Bays	
24.	1 a.m.	Relief complete.	
		Two men slightly wounded	[illegible]
		H.Q. A and B Coys went to Bde H.Q. at ECOLE de BIENFAISANCE, YPRES.	
		C and D into G.H.Q. line of trenches by TUILERIES	[illegible]
	3 a.m.	At 3 am gas fumes arrived. Companies stood to with respirators. Heavy shelling with gas shells.	[illegible]
	4.30 a.m.	Moved into cellars at Bde H.Q.	[illegible]
	12.20 pm	Under instructions from 83rd Bde, Capt Bond with C and D Companies ordered to reinforce	

1247 W 3299 200,000 (E) 8/14 J.B.C. & A. Forms/C. 2118/11.

Instructions regarding War Diaries and Intelligence Summaries are contained in F. S. Regs., Part II. and the Staff Manual respectively. Title pages will be prepared in manuscript.

WAR DIARY
or
~~INTELLIGENCE SUMMARY~~
(Erase heading not required.)

Army Form C. 2118.

10.

Hour, Date, Place	Summary of Events and Information	Remarks and references to Appendices
May 24	4th D. G's in a line about 200x South of MENIN Road facing North in Square I 17 a & b.	[illegible]
4.30 pm	High explosive shell hit building where B Coy was.	[illegible]
	2/Lt Walters and 2/Lt Evans wounded	[illegible]
	Other ranks killed 11. wounded 25	
11.30 pm	2/Lt Steyer went sick.	[illegible]
25.	H.Q. A & B Coys at Bde H.Q.	
	H.Q. A & B Coys at Bde H.Q. C and D Coys in dugouts in Sanctuary Wood	[illegible]
10 am	Two men of A wounded by shell.	[illegible]
	Five - - - C and D wounded	
	Battn relieved 5th Kings own in trenches 9. 10. 11. 12.	
	on our right 2nd K.O.	[illegible]
	on left 3rd Monmouths	

Instructions regarding War Diaries and Intelligence Summaries are contained in F. S. Regs., Part II. and the Staff Manual respectively. Title pages will be prepared in manuscript.

WAR DIARY
or
~~INTELLIGENCE SUMMARY~~

(Erase heading not required.)

Army Form C. 2118.

11.

Hour, Date, Place		Summary of Events and Information	Remarks and references to Appendices
May 26	1 a.m	Relief complete	Sct
		Headquarters in dugout about 500x behind firing line.	
		A. B. C. D and 8 M.G's in firing line	Sct
		1 M. G. in supporting point.	
		Trenches good. About 6 to 7 feet deep, with banquettes	Sct
		Germans about 300x to 400x away.	
		Situation normal all day.	Sct
		C. O and 2nd in command visited trenches	
	11 a.m	at 11 a.m	
	10.30 p.m	Warned by Bde to be ready for gas in the morning. All companies warned and respirators damped.	Sct

1247 W 3299 200,000 (E) 8/14 J.B.C. & A. Forms/C. 2118/11.

WAR DIARY
or
~~INTELLIGENCE SUMMARY~~
(Erase heading not required.)

Army Form C. 2118.

12

Hour, Date, Place	Summary of Events and Information	Remarks and references to Appendices
May 27.	Situation normal all day	F.C.T.
28	Situation normal all day.	F.C.T.
4.30 am	CO visited trenches	
12.30 pm	Trenches shelled with whizz bangs. A little damage done to the parapet. No casualties.	F.C.T.
5.30 pm	Trenches shelled with shrapnell.	F.C.T.
9.15 pm	Adjutant visited trenches.	
29. 3 a.m.	Adjutant visited trenches.	
5 a.m.	Situation normal.	
4.30 pm	Brigadier visited Battalion H.Q. 2 Lieuts Brooke, Bond, Bentall and Wilson arrived and were sent up to trenches with rations and went back to transport. Capt Mallison went back to transport.	F.C.T. F.C.T.
8 pm	Heavy shelling heard apparently north of YPRES. This was afterwards heard to be the French attacking.	F.C.T.

1247 W 3299 200,000 (E) 8/14 J.B.C. & A. Forms/C. 2118/11.

Instructions regarding War Diaries and Intelligence Summaries are contained in F. S. Regs., Part II. and the Staff Manual respectively. Title pages will be prepared in manuscript.

WAR DIARY
or
~~INTELLIGENCE SUMMARY~~
(Erase heading not required.)

Army Form C. 2118.

13.

Hour, Date, Place	Summary of Events and Information	Remarks and references to Appendices
May 30	Situation normal all day.	E.P.
2.30 am	C.O. visited the trenches.	E.P.
12.30 pm	Trenches shelled with whizz-bangs. No harm done.	
2.15 pm	Adjutant visited trenches.	
10.30 pm	11 Red flares seen apparently South of MENIN Road in direction of WITTEPOORT Farm. Reported to Bde.	E.P.
31. 1 am	Rapid fire on our left. Companies stood to. On enquiry it was found to be cavalry practising rapid.	E.P.
		E.P.
9.30 am	Adjutant visited trenches. During the morning H.Q. and MENIN ROAD were shelled from the South.	E.P.
5 pm	Situation normal.	
9 pm	One officer and one N.C.O. per Coy [illegible] [illegible] line of trenches from I 16 b to [illegible]	E.P.
11.30 pm	Returned 11.30 pm	

E. Heathcote Major
C.O. 1 K.O.Y.L.I.

1247 W 3299 200,000 (E) 8/14 J.B.C. & A. Forms/C. 2118/11.

83rd Bde.
28th Div.

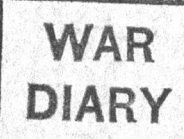

WAR
DIARY

1st K. O. Y. L. I.

J U N E

1 9 1 5

On His Majesty's Service.

Army Form C. 2118.

Instructions regarding War Diaries and Intelligence Summaries are contained in F. S. Regs., Part II. and the Staff Manual respectively. Title pages will be prepared in manuscript.

WAR DIARY
or
~~INTELLIGENCE SUMMARY~~
(Erase heading not required.)

Hour, Date, Place	Summary of Events and Information	Remarks and references to Appendices
June		
1st 2.15 a.m	Adjutant visited trenches.	J.e.S.
5 a.m	Situation normal. Wind N.N.E.	J.e.S.
12 noon	Wind N.N.E.	J.e.S.
4.30 p.m	Officers of 1st Northumberland Fusiliers visited trenches.	J.e.S.
5 p.m	Situation normal.	J.e.S.
5.30 p.m	Wind N.N.E.	
6 p.m.	Trenches shelled with whizz bangs. Six men slightly wounded.	J.e.S.
9 p.m	2 Lieuts Marshall, Bond, Robinson and Steele and no 2 C.O per Coy sent to reconnoitre G.H.Q. line of trenches.	J.e.S.
11.30 p.m	Returned from reconnaissance.	J.e.S.
2nd 1.50 a.m	Aeroplane nationality unknown dropped lights over German trenches in wood opposite our trenches.	J.e.S.
8 a.m	Situation normal. Wind N.E.	J.e.S.
	Hooge bombarded all day.	J.e.S.
5 p.m	Situation normal.	
9.45 p.m	1st Northumberland Fusiliers arrived to relieve Battn in trenches.	J.e.S.

1247 W 3299 200,000 (E) 8/14 J.B.C. & A. Forms/C. 2118/11.

Army Form C. 2118.

WAR DIARY
or
~~INTELLIGENCE SUMMARY~~
(Erase heading not required.)

Instructions regarding War Diaries and Intelligence Summaries are contained in F. S. Regs., Part II. and the Staff Manual respectively. Title pages will be prepared in manuscript.

Hour, Date, Place		Summary of Events and Information	Remarks and references to Appendices
June 3rd.	1 a.m.	Relief complete. Battalion marched by companies to SAPPERTOWN huts on VLAMERTINGHE – OUDERDOM road.	JCT
	2.30 p.m.	Battalion with transport marched to billets at WINNIEZEELE by POPERINGHE and WATOU.	JCT
	8 p.m	Arrived at billets.	JCT
4th	2 p.m	Captain Mallinson, Capt Jewors, Lieut & Quartermaster F.C. Brasier proceeded on leave.	JCT
5th	2.30 p.m	Brigadier General Ravenshaw commanding 83rd Bde inspected drafts of Battn which had arrived since May 22nd. Numbers 153 and 113.	JCT
6th.		Battalion exercised under company arrangements in close order drill, trench digging, erecting wire entanglements. Two grenadier platoons formed under 2Lieut Robinson.	JCT
	8 p.m	Draft of 130 other ranks with 2Lieuts Simpson and Burge arrived.	JCT
8th	5 p.m	2Lieut R. O. Eckersley S.W.B. left to join 1st S.W.B	JCT

Instructions regarding War Diaries and Intelligence Summaries are contained in F. S. Regs., Part II. and the Staff Manual respectively. Title pages will be prepared in manuscript.

WAR DIARY

or

~~INTELLIGENCE SUMMARY~~

(Erase heading not required.)

Army Form C. 2118.

Hour, Date, Place	Summary of Events and Information	Remarks and references to Appendices
June 9th WINNEZEELE	Capt McLennon, Capt Tewors, Lt and 2nd Lt T. C. Brance returned from leave	TCT
10th 11 a.m.	2Lt C. T. Stewitt S.W.B. left to join 1st Battn S.W.B.	TCT
	Lieut Bradley Williams took over command of C Coy.	TCT
	2Lt Marshall took over duties of Machine Gun Office.	TCT
	2Lt Wilson took over duties of Transport Office	TCT
8 pm	17 men of B Coy wounded by a bomb accident	TCT
11th 4 p.m.	Battalion route march at 4 p.m.	TCT
7.30 pm	Returned 7.30 p.m	TCT
	Captain H. A. Law arrived and took over command of A Coy.	TCT
13th	Church parade.	
	Two men rejoined battalion from Military prison HAVRE.	TCT

Instructions regarding War Diaries and Intelligence Summaries are contained in F. S. Regs., Part II. and the Staff Manual respectively. Title pages will be prepared in manuscript.

WAR DIARY

or

~~INTELLIGENCE SUMMARY~~

(Erase heading not required.)

Army Form C. 2118.

Hour, Date, Place		Summary of Events and Information	Remarks and references to Appendices
June 14th	1.30 pm	Battalion marched into huts on ZEVECOTEN – LA CLYTTE road about 400x N.W. of LA CLYTTE. Route WINNIEZEELE – WATOU – POPERINGHE – RENINGHELST – LA CLYTTE	TeJ
	6.20 pm	Arrived at huts. Battalion reported present.	TeJ
15th LA CLYTTE	9 pm.	Under instructions from Brigade Battalion fell in on alarm post.	TeJ
		Battalion and transport reported present.	TeJ
	9.25 pm	Battalion exercised under company commanders.	TeJ
16th		Battalion came on duty. Paraded under company	TeJ
	6 pm	Battalion officers.	
17th		Battalion on duty.	TeJ
	1.30 pm	Lieut Colonel W. M. Withycombe C.M.G. and Capt R. F. Day 2nd K.O.Y.L.I. visited the Battn	TeJ
	3.45 pm	Equitation class for officers.	TeJ
	6 pm	Battalion came off duty.	TeJ
18th	6 am	Sergeant Majors parade.	TeJ
	8.30 am	Companies at disposal of company commanders.	TeJ
	12 noon	equitation class for officers.	TeJ

1247 W 3299 200,000 (E) 8/14 J.B.C. & A. Forms/C. 2118/11.

Instructions regarding War Diaries and Intelligence Summaries are contained in F. S. Regs., Part II. and the Staff Manual respectively. Title pages will be prepared in manuscript.

WAR DIARY

or

~~INTELLIGENCE SUMMARY~~

(Erase heading not required.)

Army Form C. 2118.

Hour, Date, Place		Summary of Events and Information	Remarks and references to Appendices
18th. LA CLYTTE	4 p.m.	Route March under Coy arrangements.	[illegible]
19th.		Usual inspections.	[illegible]
	12 noon	Equitation class for officers.	[illegible]
	9.30 p.m.	Battalion left for KEMMEL Bivouac.	[illegible]
	11.15 p.m.	Battalion arrived at Bivouacs. Guards posted.	[illegible]
20th. KEMMEL BIVOUAC	10.20 a.m.	C.O and Capt [illegible] visited Bivouacs.	[illegible]
	3 p.m.	6th Sherwood Foresters left.	
	9 p.m.	2 officers and 100 men of B Coy working under R.E.	[illegible]
	9 p.m.	A fatigue party of 30 men of B Coy left to work under 139th Bde Mining Section.	[illegible]
	9.30 p.m.	A Coy left to occupy Subsidiary line.	[illegible]
	9.35 p.m.	C Coy — — —	[illegible]
	9.40 p.m.	D — — —	[illegible]
		Two hours work was done in improving the trenches.	[illegible]
		Companies then returned	[illegible]
21st.		Usual inspections.	[illegible]
	11.30 a.m.	C.O visited bivouacs	[illegible]
	9.30 p.m.	Party of 200 men working on subsidiary line	[illegible]
		40 men as carrying party for 139th Bde Mining Coy	[illegible]

WAR DIARY

or

~~INTELLIGENCE SUMMARY~~

(Erase heading not required.)

Instructions regarding War Diaries and Intelligence Summaries are contained in F. S. Regs., Part II. and the Staff Manual respectively. Title pages will be prepared in manuscript.

Army Form C. 2118.

Hour, Date, Place	Summary of Events and Information	Remarks and references to Appendices
June KEMMEL BIVOUACS	Usual inspections	[illegible]
22. 12.30 pm	C.O visited C & D Coy bivouacs	[illegible]
9 pm	party of 200 men left to work on Subsidiary line	[illegible]
	party of 100 men as working party for E. Yorks	[illegible]
	party of 40 men as carrying party for 135th Bde	
	party of Mining Coy	
23. 9.30 am	Capt Law, Capt Cuffe-Blumlee, Lieut Bradley, McCallum, 2Lieut Marshall and 2Lt Heath reconnoitred the E. Yorks trenches.	[illegible]
9.15 pm	Battalion marched off from Bivouacs to relieve 2nd E. Yorks, in trenches H3–K1.	[illegible]
	Transport returned to huts at LA CLYTTE	[illegible]
24. 12.27 am.	Relief complete.	[illegible]
4.30 am	Situation normal, wind left S.W.	[illegible]
9 am	Sick wastage 4.	[illegible]
10.30 am	C.O and Captain McCallum visited the trenches	[illegible]
4 pm	Situation normal. wind S.W.	[illegible]
	Brigadier General Fenwick C.M.G. visited Batt H.Q. and trenches.	[illegible]

1247 W 3299 200,000 (E) 8/14 J.B.C. & A. Forms/C. 2118/11.

Army Form C. 2118.

WAR DIARY
or
~~INTELLIGENCE SUMMARY~~
(Erase heading not required.)

Instructions regarding War Diaries and Intelligence Summaries are contained in F. S. Regs., Part II. and the Staff Manual respectively. Title pages will be prepared in manuscript.

Hour, Date, Place	Summary of Events and Information	Remarks and references to Appendices
June 24. 12 noon	Situation normal. Casualties nil.	LCJ
9 p.m.	One company 5th King's Own Regiment, strength 2 officers and 104 men, relieved 9th D.L.I. in H.1 and H.2 trenches. This company came under command of Major C. E. Bradbrooke D.S.O. O.C. Right Section.	LCJ
25. 12.5 a.m.	Relief complete.	LCJ
	Situation normal all day.	LCJ
	Sick wastage 3.	LCJ
9 a.m.	Casualties other ranks killed two, wounded one.	LCJ
	5th King's Own attached nil.	LCJ
10 a.m.	C.O. visited trenches.	LCJ
2.30 p.m.	Adjutant visited trenches.	LCJ
9.30 p.m.	Capt [illegible] D.S.O. visited trenches	LCJ
26.	Situation normal all day.	LCJ
4.45 p.m.	Mining operations by enemy reported to be taking place against J.3 right and J.3 new. Expert was sent to listen but heard nothing.	LCJ
	Sick wastage two.	LCJ

Instructions regarding War Diaries and Intelligence Summaries are contained in F. S. Regs., Part II. and the Staff Manual respectively. Title pages will be prepared in manuscript.

WAR DIARY

or

~~INTELLIGENCE SUMMARY~~

(Erase heading not required.)

Army Form C. 2118.

Hour, Date, Place		Summary of Events and Information	Remarks and references to Appendices
26.	11am	C.O. visited trenches.	
	3pm	Adjutant visited trenches.	
	9.30pm	Capt [illegible] D.S.O. visited trenches.	
		10 men [illegible] to form Bde Mining [illegible]	
27.	12.50am	[illegible] 5th R.O. attached me.	
		Sick wastage 3.	
		[illegible] all day.	
	9.45am	C.O. visited trenches	
		Casualty [illegible]	
	3pm	Adjutant visited trenches	
	10pm	Capt [illegible] D.S.O. visited trenches.	
		[illegible] all day.	
28.		Sick wastage. Capt [illegible] and [illegible] other ranks.	
		Casualties other ranks wounded two,	
		5th R.O. attached wounded two	
	11am	C.O. visited trenches	
	2pm	Adjutant visited trenches	

Instructions regarding War Diaries and Intelligence Summaries are contained in F. S. Regs., Part II. and the Staff Manual respectively. Title pages will be prepared in manuscript.

WAR DIARY

or

~~INTELLIGENCE SUMMARY~~

(Erase heading not required.)

Army Form C. 2118.

Hour, Date, Place	Summary of Events and Information	Remarks and references to Appendices
28. 9.30pm	Capt [illegible] [illegible] rejoined from leave.	[illegible]
29.	Situation normal all day.	[illegible]
	[illegible]	[illegible]
	[illegible]	[illegible]
	Major Sepp visited Battn H.Q.	
9pm	Sergeant Major Flanagan wounded about 9 pm and died	[illegible]
	in hospital at LA CLYTTE.	
30.	Battn relieved by 2nd E. Yorks.	[illegible]
12.30am	Relief complete.	[illegible]
	Battn marched into huts at LA CLYTTE.	
	Battn marched [illegible] ranks inspected by C.O.	[illegible]
11.30am	Draft of 83 other ranks inspected by C.O.	[illegible]
	Companies exercised under Company commanders	[illegible]
	2 companies on wiring picquet.	
	Battalion washed in bath at LA CLYTTE	[illegible]
4.30pm	Battalion used rifle range at SCHERPENBERG	[illegible]
	also machine gunners.	
9pm	160 men on working and carrying parties	[illegible]

1247 W 3299 200,000 (E) 8/14 J.B.C. & A. Forms/C. 2118/11.

= 83rd Bde.
28th Div.

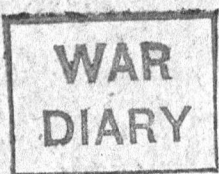

WAR DIARY

1st K. O. Y. L. I.

J U L Y

1 9 1 5

On His Majesty's Service.

Instructions regarding War Diaries and Intelligence Summaries are contained in F. S. Regs., Part II. and the Staff Manual respectively. Title pages will be prepared in manuscript.

WAR DIARY
or
~~INTELLIGENCE~~ SUMMARY
(Erase heading not required.)

Army Form C. 2118.

	Hour, Date, Place	Summary of Events and Information	Remarks and references to Appendices
July	LA CLYTTE	Usual inspections	
		Riding class for officers.	
1st	11 a.m.	Brigadier General Rawlinson visited the camp	E.S.
2nd		Lt Col [illegible] Major [illegible] and Captain [illegible] Bde	E.S.
		[illegible] 6th KOYLI visited the Battalion.	E.S.
3rd 4th		Usual inspections and officers equitation class.	E.S.
4th	11 a.m.	Sir Charles Fergusson Cmdg 2nd Corps visited Battalion	
5th	Trenches. 9 p.m.	Battalion and 2 coys 5th K.O. attached relieved 2nd	E.S.
		E. Yorks and 2 Coys 5th K.O. in trenches, Right sector	
		2Lt Tomkins came to Battn H.Q. to learn the	E.S.
		duties of Adjutant.	
	11.45 pm	Received warning from Bde that there would probably be heavy gun firing to the [illegible] about 5.30 a.m 6th. Information sent to Coys.	E.S.
	12 m.n.	Relief complete.	E.S.
6th	4.30 a.m	Situation normal. Wind light S.W. Foggy.	E.S.
		patrol sent from H.4 to crater reported no signs of hostile activity, as reported by 2nd East Yorks.	E.S.
	9 a.m	Sick wastage nil.	E.S.

1247 W 3299 200,000 (E) 8/14 J.B.C. & A. Forms/C. 2118/11.

Instructions regarding War Diaries and Intelligence Summaries are contained in F. S. Regs., Part II. and the Staff Manual respectively. Title pages will be prepared in manuscript.

WAR DIARY
or
~~INTELLIGENCE SUMMARY~~
(Erase heading not required.)

Army Form C. 2118.

2

Hour, Date, Place	Summary of Events and Information	Remarks and references to Appendices
July 6th TRENCHES		
9.45 a.m	C.O and 2nd in command (Capt R. McElkin D.S.O). visited trenches.	R.P.
10.30 a.m	Situation normal. Wind Fresh S.W.	R.P.
	Lieut R. Boys-Stones 9th D.L.I. reported at Battn H.Q for instruction in duties of Adjutant.	R.P.
12 noon	Casualty. one other ranks wounded slightly at duty.	R.P.
	Adjutant & Lt Boys-Stones visited trenches	R.P.
2 p.m.	Brigadier General Rawenshaw visited Battn H.Q.	R.P.
4.15 pm	after going round trenches.	R.P.
	Situation normal. Wind fresh S.W.	R.P.
4.30 pm	2nd in command visited trenches.	R.P.
10.30 pm	J3 right trench mortared.	R.P.
11.45 pm	Situation normal. Wind fresh S.W.	
7th 4.30 a.m	Rapid rifle fire against K1 and J3 left at intervals during the night for no apparent reason.	R.P.
	Patrols and Snipers out along all the front but found nothing.	R.P.
10 a.m	C.O and Adjutant visited trenches.	R.P.

1247 W 3299 200,000 (E) 8/14 J.B.C. & A. Forms/C. 2118/11.

Instructions regarding War Diaries and Intelligence Summaries are contained in F. S. Regs., Part II. and the Staff Manual respectively. Title pages will be prepared in manuscript.

WAR DIARY

or

~~INTELLIGENCE SUMMARY~~

(Erase heading not required.)

Army Form C. 2118.

3

Hour, Date, Place		Summary of Events and Information	Remarks and references to Appendices
	TRENCHES.		
July 7th.	12 noon	Casualties other ranks killed 2. wounded one.	[illegible]
	4.30 pm	Crumps on E. Slope of KEMMEL HILL.	[illegible]
	6.30 pm	Capt Follett Bde Major visited Battn H.Q.	[illegible]
	9.40 pm	2nd in command and Lt Boys Stoner visited trenches	[illegible]
	11.30 pm	Trench mortars into T3. Right.	[illegible]
8th	4.30 am	Situation normal. Wind light. S.W.	[illegible]
	9 am	Sick wastage one.	[illegible]
	11.15 am	C.O, adjutant and Lt Boys Stoner visited trenches	[illegible]
	12 noon	Casualties. 2Lt W. D. BENTALL 1st KOYLI wounded not serious. other ranks killed by rifle grenade one wounded 3.	[illegible]
	4 pm	Brigadier General Ravenshaw visited trenches and Battn H.Q.	[illegible]
	7.30 pm	T1 and T3 right trench mortared. Artillery replied effectively.	[illegible]
	9.45 pm	2nd in command visited trenches.	[illegible]

Army Form C. 2118.

4

Instructions regarding War Diaries and Intelligence Summaries are contained in F. S. Regs., Part II. and the Staff Manual respectively. Title pages will be prepared in manuscript.

WAR DIARY
or
~~INTELLIGENCE SUMMARY~~

(Erase heading not required.)

Hour, Date, Place		Summary of Events and Information	Remarks and references to Appendices
	TRENCHES		R.P.
July 9th		Situation normal. Wind light S.W.	
	4.30 a.m	Bunker mine from F3 left exploded. Two craters	R.P.
	5.30 am	formed.	
		Sick wastage nil. Emergency telephone wire to	
	9 a m	20 men bringing up	R.P.
		trenches. Working all day.	
		2Lt Tomkin returned to duty with A Coy.	R.P.
	10.15 am	Adjutant visited trenches.	
		C.O. visited trenches	R.P.
	10.30 am	Casualties. Other ranks killed 3. Wounded 10.	
	12 noon	Due to enemy trench mortars.	R.P.
		2nd in Command visited trenches.	R.P.
	9.30 pm	Situation normal. Light west wind.	R.P.
10th	4.30 a.m	C.O. visited trenches.	R.P.
	10.15 a.m	Brigadier General Rawenshaw visited Batt^n H.Q.	R.P.
	11.15 am	Casualties. Other ranks wounded 4.	R.P.
	12 noon	Col Bare G.S.O.1 22nd Division conducted round	
	4 pm	the subsidiary line by Captain Hallinton.	R.P.

1247 W 3299 200,000 (E) 8/14 J.B.C. & A. Forms/C. 2118/11.

Army Form C. 2118.

5

Instructions regarding War Diaries and Intelligence Summaries are contained in F. S. Regs., Part II. and the Staff Manual respectively. Title pages will be prepared in manuscript.

WAR DIARY
or
~~INTELLIGENCE SUMMARY~~

(Erase heading not required.)

Hour, Date, Place	Summary of Events and Information	Remarks and references to Appendices
Feby 10th TRENCHES	Situation normal. French mortars on T3. Left	R.P.
4.30pm	enemy reported by Bde Mining Section to be making	R.P.
6.55pm	a mine under T3 Right and T3 New.	R.P.
8.30pm	Mining under T3 Right confirmed. Preparations made to explode a charge down bore hole in T3 right. 2nd in command went up to T3 right.	R.P.
10.55pm	Charge of 30 lbs exploded; crater formed 10 foot deep in centre.	R.P.
	New bore hole sunk for listening.	R.P.
	Explosion was followed by rapid fire from enemy trenches; afterwards all quiet.	R.P.
11th 4.30am	Situation normal. Light [illegible] Co.	R.P.
9am	Sick wastage one.	R.P.
10am	C.O visited trenches.	R.P.
12 noon	Casualties wounded other ranks two.	R.P.
4.30pm	A few French mortars, otherwise all quiet.	R.P.
	Battalion relieved by 2nd E. Yorks.	R.P.
11.50pm	Relief completed.	R.P.

1247 W 3299 200,000 (E) 8/14 J.B.C. & A. Forms/C. 2118/11.

Instructions regarding War Diaries and Intelligence Summaries are contained in F. S. Regs., Part II. and the Staff Manual respectively. Title pages will be prepared in manuscript.

WAR DIARY or ~~INTELLIGENCE~~ SUMMARY

(Erase heading not required.)

Army Form C. 2118.

6

Hour, Date, Place	Summary of Events and Information	Remarks and references to Appendices
LA CLYTTE		
12th	Usual inspections and Coy Officers parades	C.P.
2.30 pm	C.O left for 5 days leave to England.	C.P.
	Captain Mallinson D.S.O. in command.	C.P.
13th 3 pm	Brigade Horse Show. Won by 1st KOSB.	C.P.
14th 2 pm	Sergeant Major Miller, C.S.M. Thirley, Sergeant [illegible], Cpl [illegible] and L/c Rowland went on leave	C.P.
8.30 pm	Heavy gun fire and rapid rifle fire heard.	
	Battalion ordered to fall in. Turned out in 35 minutes	C.P.
9.10 pm	C.O reported to Bde HQ and ordered to stand by.	C.P.
12 mn	Battalion ordered to fall out.	C.P.
	This was apparently caused by Germans exploding a mine in front of E.1. trench. They did not attack.	C.P.
15th	Usual inspections and parades. Battalion exercised on rifle range at SCHERPENBERG.	C.P.
	Capt Mallinson, Capt [illegible], Capt Law and Lt Bradley Williams visited artillery observation posts on KEMMEL HILL.	C.P.
16th	Usual inspections and parades.	C.P.
	Capt G.R. Bond and Capt [illegible] Blundell visited KEMMEL HILL	C.P.

Instructions regarding War Diaries and Intelligence Summaries are contained in F. S. Regs., Part II. and the Staff Manual respectively. Title pages will be prepared in manuscript.

WAR DIARY
or
~~INTELLIGENCE SUMMARY~~

(Erase heading not required.)

Army Form C. 2118.

2

Hour, Date, Place		Summary of Events and Information	Remarks and references to Appendices
	LA CLYTTE.		
16th.		2Lt A. J. Pick D.L.I. attached [illegible] Left Battn to join Bde Mining Section.	T.S.
17th		Usual inspections. B.C.D in trenches.	T.S.
		Battn relieved 1st & 2nd in trenches.	T.S.
		A in reserve.	T.S.
	8 pm.	Battn left LA CLYTTE at 8pm	T.S.
	10.25pm	Relief complete.	T.S.
	11 pm	Capt Mallinson visited trenches.	
			T.S.
18th	Trenches. 9 am	Sick wastage nil.	T.S.
	9.30 am	Capt Mallinson visited trenches. Adjutant	
	10.15 am	103rd Battery had a premature burst. Slightly wounded at	
		hit by fuse in Battn H.Q.	T.S.
		duty.	
	10.45 am	Lt Col C. E. Heathcote D.S.O. returned to Battn H.Q.	T.S.
		from leave.	
		Casualties other ranks. Killed one, wounded three.	T.S.
	12 noon	Brigadier visited Battn H.Q.	T.S.
	4 pm	Capt Mallinson visited trenches.	T.S.
	10 pm	Situation normal all day.	T.S.

1247 W 3299 200,000 (E) 8/14 J.B.C. & A. Forms/C. 2118/11.

Instructions regarding War Diaries and Intelligence Summaries are contained in F. S. Regs., Part II. and the Staff Manual respectively. Title pages will be prepared in manuscript.

WAR DIARY
or
~~INTELLIGENCE SUMMARY~~

(Erase heading not required.)

Army Form C. 2118.

81

Hour, Date, Place		Summary of Events and Information	Remarks and references to Appendices
July	TRENCHES.		
19th	10 a.m	C.O and Adjutant visited trenches.	P.S.T.
	12 noon	Casualties. other ranks wounded one.	P.S.T.
	6.30 pm	Germans opened rapid rifle fire at one of our aeroplanes.	P.S.T.
	10 pm	Capt Mallinson visited trenches.	P.S.T.
		Situation normal all day.	P.S.T.
			P.S.T.
		Sick wastage three.	P.S.T.
20th	9 a.m	C.O and Adjutant visited trenches	
	10.15 am	Brigadier visited Batt^n H.Q.	P.S.T.
	4.15 pm	Lt. Bradley Williams wounded. Flesh wound in left thigh; left arm broken. Caused by one bullet	P.S.T.
	6 pm	Second in Command visited trenches.	P.S.T.
	9.45 pm	Situation normal all day.	
			P.S.T.
21st		Sick wastage one.	P.S.T.
	9 a.m	Adjutant visited trenches.	P.S.T.
	10.30 am	C.O visited observation post on KEMMEL HILL	
	11.30 am	Casualties. Other ranks killed one wounded [illegible]	P.S.T.
	12 noon		

Instructions regarding War Diaries and Intelligence Summaries are contained in F. S. Regs., Part II. and the Staff Manual respectively. Title pages will be prepared in manuscript.

Army Form C. 2118.

9

WAR DIARY
or
~~INTELLIGENCE SUMMARY~~
(Erase heading not required.)

Hour, Date, Place		Summary of Events and Information	Remarks and references to Appendices
July 21st	TRENCHES		
	4.30 pm	General Boles cmdg 84th Bde and C.R.E. 28th Div visited Battn H.Q.	[illegible]
		C Company took over K2, K2.A, K1.A trenches.	[illegible]
	9 pm	B and D expanded to occupy the original line	[illegible]
	11 pm	Capt Mallinson visited trenches.	[illegible]
		Situation normal all day.	[illegible]
		C.O and Adjutant visited trenches	[illegible]
22nd	10 am	Casualty. Other ranks killed one, wounded three	[illegible]
	12 noon	Capt Mallinson visited trenches.	[illegible]
	10 pm	Situation normal all day.	[illegible]
		Adjutant visited trenches.	[illegible]
23rd	10.15 am	Casualties other ranks killed one, wounded one	[illegible]
	12 noon	Battn relieved by 1st [illegible]	[illegible]
	10.30 pm	Relief complete 10.30 pm. After relief Battn marched into bivouacs near SCHERPENBERG.	[illegible]
24th	SCHERPENBERG.	Usual inspections.	
		Capt H.A. Law and Lieut Wells RAMC proceeded on leave.	[illegible]

1247 W 3299 200,000 (E) 8/14 J.B.C. & A. Forms/C. 2118/11.

Army Form C. 2118. 10

Instructions regarding War Diaries and Intelligence Summaries are contained in F. S. Regs., Part II. and the Staff Manual respectively. Title pages will be prepared in manuscript.

WAR DIARY
or
~~INTELLIGENCE SUMMARY~~
(Erase heading not required.)

Hour, Date, Place		Summary of Events and Information	Remarks and references to Appendices
July 25th	SCHERPENBERG	Church parade.	
	9.30 am	Brigadier General Ravenshaw inspected the last two drafts.	
26th		Usual inspections and company parades. Battalion exercised in musketry on the SCHERPENBERG range.	
27th	3.15 pm	C.O. inspected companies in marching order.	
	7.45 pm	Lt Wilson, 2Lt Robson and two other ranks (joined?). C Company relieved 2nd KOs in reserve for left Sector at SANDBAG VILLA.	
28th	3 pm	2nd in Command inspected headquarters and machine gunners in marching order.	
29th		Usual inspections and parades.	
30th	8 pm	Battn with 2 platoons 6th Dorsets, 2 " 7th E Yorks, 1 company 7th Yorkshire Regt } attached. relieved 5th Kings Own with one company 1st 4th L	

1247 W 3299 200,000 (E) 8/14 J.B.C. & A. Forms/C. 2118/11.

11

Instructions regarding War Diaries and Intelligence Summaries are contained in F. S. Regs., Part II. and the Staff Manual respectively. Title pages will be prepared in manuscript.

WAR DIARY

or

~~INTELLIGENCE SUMMARY~~.

(*Erase heading not required.*)

Army Form C. 2118.

	Hour, Date, Place	Summary of Events and Information	Remarks and references to Appendices
	TRENCHES	attached in the left sector	L.P.
July 30	11.35 pm	Relief complete 11.35 pm	L.P.
		A, B, and D in the firing line. C in reserve.	
	11 pm	2nd in command visited trenches.	
31.		Situation normal all day.	L.P.
		Casualty other ranks wounded one.	L.P.
	10 a.m	C.O visited trenches	
	6.30 pm	Received message from Brigade that attached troops would be withdrawn.	L.P.
		Two platoons of C company sent up in support to A.	L.P.
	10.45 pm	Changes in dispositions complete.	L.P.
	11. pm	2nd in command visited trenches.	L.P.

(73989) W4141—463. 400,000. 9/14. H.&J.Ltd. Forms/C. 2118/10.

Remarks on <u>Draft joined</u> 20-8-15

22117 L/Cpl A W Hunt
9970 Pte F. Carr.
5261 Pte J Cairns
10458 Pte G Streeter
20940 L/Cpl C Whitcroft
10125 Pte E Roberts
21222 Pte S Brampton
21074 Pte R G Collins

(Sick or Wounded rejoined from Base & England)

23156 Pte B F Hall 3rd Bn. enlisted 17-3-15 left England 6-7-15 since at Base since

21993 Pte J Carr 3rd Bn. enlisted 8-3-15 left England about 25 July been at Base since.

21940 Pte A Baxter, 3rd Bn. enlisted 11-3-15, left England about 25 July been at Base since

22046 Pte A Gray enlisted 6-9-14 11th Hussars, transferred to 3rd K.O.Y.L.I. with Cavalry draft

21818 Pte G Goodall 3rd Bn. enlisted 25-3-15, left England about 21-7-15 been at Base since in hospital with abscess on back

No. ~~[illegible]~~ 10750 Pte L. McCrone.
enlisted 19 Nov 14.9.14 transferred
to 3rd Bn for Home Service only,
[illegible] on 1.5.15 (on
own statement) Left Employment
admitted 8-7-15 Remained the Battn.
[illegible]. Age 46 [illegible].

7226 [?] Pte H Darcy, 8th Bn.
enlisted 1-4-15 [?]
admitted the 21.7.15 Left Employment
at the Battn. Remaining [illegible]
[illegible] PB (permanent Base
duty) on [illegible] of
[illegible] [illegible] [illegible] of [illegible]

15961 Pte Hayward, 1st Bn to 3rd Bn in April 1915, slight rupture owing to motor accident, all right now. Age 36.

21876 Pte Clifton 3rd Bn. Age 41. enlisted 1-3-15.

21815 Pte Remington 3rd Bn. Age 39. enlisted 23-3-15.

16903 Pte Hughes, Transferred from 9th Bn to 3rd Bn. April 15. Does not know why he was transferred. Age 46. N.B.G.

12[illegible] Pte Frost, transferred from 10th Bn. to 3rd Bn 1-5-15, he does not know why he was transferred, age 47. N.B.G.

21974 Pte Crossland 3rd Bn Age 30 enlisted 6-3-15.

N[redacted].G. = No [redacted] Good.

2991 Pte Cross. 3rd Bn. Age 23 enlisted 8-3-15.

2996 Pte Coleman 3rd Bn. Age 39 enlisted 3-8-15

664 Pte Halkyard transferred from 12th Bn to 3rd Bn. 1st May. 15. For Home Service only. no idea why. Age 26. N.

1218 Pte Wright transferred from 12th Bn. to 3rd Bn. 1-5-15, he has no idea why? Age 42. N. G.

2198 Pte Dennis 3rd Bn. Age 33 enlisted 8-3-15.

788 Pte Wilson transferred from 12th Bn to 3rd Bn 1-5-15 for Home Service only. Could not account. Had leg broken before enlisting & a piece of bone removed from the shin. Age 29.

479 Pte Dubery transferred from 12 Bn to 3rd Bn. 1-5-15, he has no idea why? Age 36. N. G.

Copy

M 432

M.O.
1st K.O.Y.L.I.

These men on attached list will be sent down country for duty on lines of Communication under regimental arrangements.

10.8.15

Sd. H. S. Roch
Lt Col R.A.M.C.
D.A.D.M.S. 28th Div

Copy 1st K.O.Y.L.I.

A.D.M.S.
28th Div.
10.8.15
M/425.

No.	Rank &	Name.		Age.	Disability	Remarks.
3118	Pte.	Brannan	D	22	Deformed right arm result of old fracture.	To be sent to Base for duty on L of C.
19912	"	Horton	W.	43	Pyorrhoea Dyspepsia and loss of sight.	Do.
14415	"	Carter	J.	45	Asthma	Do
739	"	Edwards	H.W.	50	Deformed right foot	Do.
19244	"	Hastelow	E.	38.	Chronic inflammation of left knee joint.	Do.

11.8.15

[illegible] in Draft, [illegible] 5-8-15

6[illegible] Pte W. Turner. Transferred from 12th Bn. to 3rd Bn. on 1-5-15, as unfit for active service owing to V. vein left leg. Age 28.

---

786 Pte Whitfield transferred from 12th Bn. to 3rd Bn. 1-5-15 for Home Defence only. Age 44.

---

666 Pte Hudson. Transferred from 12th Bn. to 3rd Bn. 1-5-15. Alleged complaint [illegible] [illegible] [illegible]. Age 35.

16547 Pte Hazelgreaves transferred from 12th Bn. to 3rd Bn. January 1915, in consequence of Rheumatism in knees, fit for home service only. Age 38.

17830 Pte Field. Transferred from 12th Bn. to 3rd Bn. April 1915, in consequence of being flat footed & unable to march & fit for home service only. 35

19192 Pte Lysack. Transferred from 11th Bn. to 3rd Bn. about May 1915, owing to deafness. 29.

Copy To the [illegible] Commanding
1st Batt [illegible]

[illegible]

4/9/15 [illegible]

Major [illegible]

SCALE 1/5000
From VIERSTRAAT
M.1.
L.7C
L.7.B
L.7.A
L5
L6
L4
L3
L2
K3
DP
L.1.
K2B
K2A
K2
K1B
D.P.
K.1.A
K1 DP
K1
PETIT BOIS
H4
H2
H1

Ref. map Sheet 28. YPRES

Scale 1/40,000.

Squares N 18
24

83rd Bde.
28th Div.

WAR
DIARY

1st K. O. Y. L. I.

A U G U S T

1 9 1 5

On His Majesty's Service.

Army Form C. 2118.

Instructions regarding War Diaries and Intelligence Summaries are contained in F. S. Regs., Part II. and the Staff Manual respectively. Title pages will be prepared in manuscript.

WAR DIARY
or
INTELLIGENCE SUMMARY.
(*Erase heading not required.*)

Hour, Date, Place		Summary of Events and Information	Remarks and references to Appendices
Aug. 1st.	TRENCHES.	MINDEN DAY. Lt Col Adams sent out roses from England, which were worn by the troops.	L.S.
		Congratulatory telegram received from Major General Bulfin C.B. G.O.C. 28th Division. Copy attached	L.S.
		Situation normal all day.	L.S.
		Casualties other ranks wounded two.	L.S.
	10.15am	C.O. and Adjutant visited trenches.	
		Draft of 20 inspected by Brigadier. Five men medically examined and found unfit.	L.S.
	3.10pm	2Lt GENT 3rd D.L.I. attached 1st KOYLI left Battalion to join Bde pioneer section.	L.S.
	4.30pm	Brigadier General Rawlinson C.M.G. visited Battn HQ.	L.S.
		2nd in Command visited trenches.	L.S.
	10.30pm	Received warning that 84th Bde were going to blow up a house in N.30.a.1 9 at 10.2 2nd	L.S.
	10.50pm	House was not blown up.	L.S.

Instructions regarding War Diaries and Intelligence Summaries are contained in F. S. Regs., Part II. and the Staff Manual respectively. Title pages will be prepared in manuscript.

WAR DIARY
or
~~INTELLIGENCE SUMMARY.~~
(Erase heading not required.)

Army Form C. 2118.

Hour, Date, Place	Summary of Events and Information	Remarks and references to Appendices
TRENCHES		
~~July~~ Aug 2.	Situation normal day.	E.P
10 am	C.O and Adjutant visited trenches.	E.P
	Casualties other ranks killed 2. wounded three.	E.P
	One of these of A Coy killed. He was recommended for gallant conduct on May 8th at FREZENBERG.	E.P
3 pm	One sergeant and 10 men left Batn to be attached to Divisional Salvage Corps.	E.P
11 pm	2nd in command visited trenches	E.P
	2nd Lieuts. Welch, Lyne and Martindale joined the Battalion and were posted to B, C, and D Coys respectively.	E.P
3rd	Situation normal all day.	E.P
10.30 am	C.O and Adjutant and Major Douglas Hutchinson R.E visited the trenches	E.P
	Casualties other ranks wounded 2.	E.P
	1st Y and L regiment relieved 2nd Cheshires on our right.	E.P
11 pm	2nd in command visited trenches	E.P
4th.	Situation normal all day.	E.P
	Casualties other ranks killed nil, wounded three	E.P
9.45 am	C.O, Adjutant, and Bde machine gun officer	

(73989) W4141—463. 400,000. 9/14. H.&J.Ltd. Forms/C. 2118/10.

Instructions regarding War Diaries and Intelligence Summaries are contained in F. S. Regs., Part II. and the Staff Manual respectively. Title pages will be prepared in manuscript.

WAR DIARY
or
~~INTELLIGENCE SUMMARY.~~
(Erase heading not required.)

Army Form C. 2118.

Hour, Date, Place	Summary of Events and Information	Remarks and references to Appendices
TRENCHES		
4th	visited trenches.	
	Ration taken up by pack ponies to K.3, also	
	Sandbags, thereby saving a lot of carrying	
11 pm	2nd in command visited trenches.	
5th	Situation normal all day.	
10 am	C.O. and Adjutant visited trenches	
	Casualties nil.	
	Brigadier visited Battn HQ.	
4 pm	draft of 19 arrived. report attached	
6th	Situation normal all day.	
	Casualties other ranks wounded 2	
	Battalion relieved by 2nd East Yorks.	
	Battalion marched to Huts	
11.20 pm	Relief complete, and Battalion	
	at SCHERPENBERG.	
7th – 12th SCHERPENBERG	Battalion resting. Company parades and inspections.	
	Very heavy carrying parties found. On three nights there were 400 men out and also 120 employed on Bde fatigues daily.	

(73989) W4141—463. 400,000. 9/14. H.&J.Ltd. Forms/C. 2118/10.

Army Form C. 2118.

4

Instructions regarding War Diaries and Intelligence Summaries are contained in F. S. Regs., Part II. and the Staff Manual respectively. Title pages will be prepared in manuscript.

WAR DIARY
or
~~INTELLIGENCE SUMMARY.~~
(*Erase heading not required.*)

Hour, Date, Place	Summary of Events and Information	Remarks and references to Appendices
August ~~June~~ 7th	Capt Hallison D.S.O. assumed command of B Coy	S.G.T
~~July~~ 7th	Capt W. S. Brooke arrived to join Battn from	
	being G.S.O. to G.O.C. VIth Corps and took over	S.G.T
	C. Coy.	
Aug ~~July~~ 12th TRENCHES.	Battalion relieved 2nd East Yorks in the ~~[illegible]~~ trenches	S.G.T
	A, B, C in the firing line. D Coy in reserve.	S.G.T
10.45 pm	Relief complete 10.45 p.m.	S.G.T
	Col Challoner 6th Leicesters came to Battn H.Q	
13th	Situation normal.	
	Casualty other ranks wounded one	S.G.T
10. am	C.O. and Col. Challoner visited trenches	S.G.T
	2 coys 6th Leicester Regt joined the Sector.	S.G.T
	1½ coys were distributed in the fire and support	
	trenches. ½ coy in reserve. C Coy North withdrew to	S.G.T
	SCHERPENBERG.	S.G.T
11.45 pm	Changes in dispositions complete 11.45 pm	
	Adjt 6th Leicesters came to Battn H.Q	S.G.T
	5 men sent to permanent base duty. See report	S.G.T

(73989) W4141—463. 400,000. 9/14. H.&J.Ltd. Forms/C. 2118/10.

Instructions regarding War Diaries and Intelligence Summaries are contained in F. S. Regs., Part II. and the Staff Manual respectively. Title pages will be prepared in manuscript.

WAR DIARY
or
~~INTELLIGENCE SUMMARY.~~
(Erase heading not required.)

Army Form C. 2118.

Hour, Date, Place		Summary of Events and Information	Remarks and references to Appendices
Aug 14.	TRENCHES	Situation normal all day	[illegible]
		Casualty KOYLI other ranks wounded one –	
		6th Leicesters other ranks wounded one.	[illegible]
	10.15 am	Brigadier General Bainbridge 110th Bde arrived at	
		Battn HQrs was shown round trenches by C.O.	[illegible]
	2 pm	K2A shelled with 16 whizz bangs. No damage.	[illegible]
	10.30 pm	Adjt. KOYLI and 6th Leicesters visited trenches.	[illegible]
15th		Situation normal all day.	
		Casualties KOYLI other ranks wounded 6 – 6th	[illegible]
		Leicesters other ranks wounded one.	
	8.30 pm	C. Coy KOYLI returned to trenches and 6th	[illegible]
		Leicesters withdrew.	
16th		Situation normal all day	
		Casualties other ranks killed one wounded 4.	[illegible]
	11 am.	Artillery tested.	
		18th Battery replied in 33 seconds.	[illegible]
		22nd " " " 8 minutes owing to	
		defects in telephone wire.	

Instructions regarding War Diaries and Intelligence Summaries are contained in F. S. Regs., Part II. and the Staff Manual respectively. Title pages will be prepared in manuscript.

WAR DIARY
or
~~INTELLIGENCE SUMMARY.~~

(*Erase heading not required.*)

Army Form C. 2118.

9

Hour, Date, Place	Summary of Events and Information	Remarks and references to Appendices
Aug 19th TRENCHES	Situation normal all day.	[illegible]
	Casualties other ranks killed nil, wounded 3.	[illegible]
8.40 am	German paper balloon dropped behind our trenches. Nothing on it. This was forwarded to Bde H.Q.	[illegible]
10 am	C.O. visited trenches.	[illegible]
4 pm	Brigadier visited Battn H.Q.	[illegible]
4.30 pm	Lt Col Mackenzie, Smith, 2 officers and 8 O.R. Yorkshire Dragoons visited Battn H.Q. and were taken round the trenches by Adjutant	[illegible]
9 pm	Heavy firing on our left. Lancashire Fusiliers (10th) had about 20 casualties from trench mortar and rifle grenades. All quiet in front of us.	[illegible]

(73989) W4141—463. 400,000. 9/14. H.&J.Ltd. Forms/C. 2118/10.

WAR DIARY
or
INTELLIGENCE SUMMARY.
(*Erase heading not required.*)

Army Form C. 2118.

Instructions regarding War Diaries and Intelligence Summaries are contained in F. S. Regs., Part II. and the Staff Manual respectively. Title pages will be prepared in manuscript.

Hour, Date, Place	Summary of Events and Information	Remarks and references to Appendices
TRENCHES		
Aug 18	Situation normal all day	[illegible]
	Casualties other ranks wounded one.	[illegible]
	Relieved by 2nd East Lancs in the trenches.	[illegible]
10.25pm	Relief complete 10.25 p.m.	
	Very quick. Machine guns were last to report	[illegible]
	Batt^n went into Huts at SCHERPENBERG	[illegible]
18-24.	Battalion in huts:	
SCHERPENBERG	Very heavy working and carrying parties found	
	On one day there were 10 officers and 595	
	other ranks out.	
	Lt W. J. Key joined Batt^n and was posted	
20.	to C Coy.	[illegible]
	Draft of 15 S.R. arrived. Regt attached	[illegible]

Instructions regarding War Diaries and Intelligence Summaries are contained in F. S. Regs., Part II. and the Staff Manual respectively. Title pages will be prepared in manuscript.

WAR DIARY
or
~~INTELLIGENCE SUMMARY.~~
(Erase heading not required.)

Army Form C. 2118.

Hour, Date, Place	Summary of Events and Information	Remarks and references to Appendices
Aug 24. TRENCHES.	Battalion relieved 2nd E. Yorks in the trenches.	GT
10 pm	Relief complete.	GT
	A, D, C in firing line. B in reserve.	
	2Lt Marshall went on leave and 2Lt Brooke took	
	charge of machine guns.	
		GT
25.	Situation normal all day.	GT
	Sick wastage 3. Casualties. O.R. wounded 2.	
10.15 am	C.O visited trenches.	GT
26th	Situation normal all day	GT
	Sick wastage nil. Casualties. O.R. killed one.	
	wounded 3.	
	2 German aeroplanes were flying over our lines	
	from 7 30 a.m till 10.40 a.m when two of our	GT
	own machines appeared.	
11 am	C.O visited trenches.	GT
12 noon	Lt Col C.R. Ingham Brooke D.S.O. rejoined Battn	GT
	to Command. Remained with Quarter master	

(73989) W4141—463. 400,000. 9/14. H.&J.Ltd. Forms/C. 2118/10.

Instructions regarding War Diaries and Intelligence Summaries are contained in F. S. Regs., Part II. and the Staff Manual respectively. Title pages will be prepared in manuscript.

WAR DIARY
or
INTELLIGENCE SUMMARY.
(*Erase heading not required.*)

Army Form C. 2118.

	Hour, Date, Place	Summary of Events and Information	Remarks and references to Appendices
27th	Trenches	Situation normal all day	[illegible]
		Sick wastage 2/Lt Tomkins and 3 O.R.	[illegible]
		Casualties O.R. killed nil. wounded one.	[illegible]
		A few whizz bangs in the trenches in the morning.	
	10 am	Major General Bulfin, Brigadier General Ravenshaw and Major Heathcote visited trenches.	[illegible]
28th		Situation normal all day.	[illegible]
		Sick wastage 2. Casualties nil.	
	10 am	C.O visited trenches.	[illegible]
	1.56 pm	Message sent to trenches to take cover in slit trenches	[illegible]
	2.8 pm	all ready.	[illegible]
	5 pm	Artillery tested. 18th Battery replied in 20 seconds. 22nd Battery in 33 seconds.	[illegible]
29th		Situation normal all day.	
		Sick wastage Capt Bond. and 3 O.R. Casualties nil.	[illegible]
	10.30 am	C.O. visited visited trenches	[illegible]

Instructions regarding War Diaries and Intelligence Summaries are contained in F. S. Regs., Part II. and the Staff Manual respectively. Title pages will be prepared in manuscript.

WAR DIARY
or
INTELLIGENCE SUMMARY
(Erase heading not required.)

Army Form C. 2118.

10

Hour, Date, Place		Summary of Events and Information	Remarks and references to Appendices
30.	TRENCHES.	Situation normal all day	
		Sick wastage nil. Casualties O.R. killed nil. wounded four. 2Lt Marshall returned and Lt Robinson went on leave	
	10.20am	C.O visited trenches	
	11 a.m	Message sent to man all trenches	
	11.14am	All ready	
		Relieved by 2nd E Yorks.	
		Relieved by [illegible] All companies finished by 9.15 pm	
	11 am	Relief complete. except left Coy, who delayed relief by losing themselves	
		Battalion went to Bivouac at SCHERPENBERG after relief	
31.	SCHERPENBERG.	Battalion resting.	
	7 pm.	600 men digging on subsidiary line	
		79 — carrying party.	
		All officers out except Headquarter Staff.	
		Lt Col. C.R. Ingham Brooke D.S.O took over command of Battn from Major (Temp Lt Col) C.S. Heathcote D.S.O	

C R Ingham Brooke –
Lt Colonel

1247 W 3299 200,000 (E) 8/14 J.B.C. & A. Forms/C. 2118/11.

83rd Bde.
28th Div.

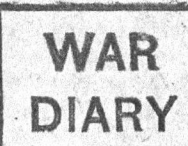

WAR
DIARY

1st K. O. Y. L. I.

S E P T E M B E R

1 9 1 5

On His Majesty's Service.

Instructions regarding War Diaries and Intelligence Summaries are contained in F. S. Regs., Part II. and the Staff Manual respectively. Title pages will be prepared in manuscript.

WAR DIARY
or
~~INTELLIGENCE SUMMARY~~
(Erase heading not required.)

Army Form C. 2118.

Hour, Date, Place		Summary of Events and Information	Remarks and references to Appendices
SCHERPENBERG			
Sept. 1st		Battn. had baths at WESTOUTRE.	S.C.T.
2nd	7pm	630 men digging on Subsidiary line	S.C.T.
		55 – carrying party	
		All officers out except H.Q. Staff	S.C.T.
		Sgt Brady and party specially complimented by R.E.	S.C.T.
4th		600 men digging on Subsidiary line	S.C.T.
		50 men carrying party.	S.C.T.
5th		Church parade	
		Lieut Robinson returned and Captain Mallinson proceeded on leave	S.C.T.
		Battn relieved 2nd East Lancs in the trenches.	S.C.T.
	10.18pm	Relief complete.	S.C.T.
6th		Situation normal. Sick wastage nil.	S.C.T.
		Casualties other ranks killed one wounded one	S.C.T.
		C.O and 2nd in Command visited trenches	S.C.T.
	10.45am		
	3pm	A/73rd Howitzer Battery registered.	
7th		Situation normal. Sick wastage Capt Mon Blundell Fever.	S.C.T.

1247 W 3299 200,000 (E) 8/14 J.B.C. & A. Forms/C. 2118/11.

31

Army Form C. 2118.

Instructions regarding War Diaries and Intelligence Summaries are contained in F. S. Regs., Part II. and the Staff Manual respectively. Title pages will be prepared in manuscript.

WAR DIARY
or
~~INTELLIGENCE SUMMARY~~.

(*Erase heading not required.*)

Date	Hour, Date, Place	Summary of Events and Information	Remarks and references to Appendices
Sept. 7.	Trenches.	Casualties. O.R. wounded 2.	R.J.
	10 am	C.O and adjutant visited trenches.	R.J.
8th		Situation normal.	R.J.
		Sick wastage one other ranks. Chill.	R.J.
		Casualties other ranks wounded one	R.J.
		Capt J. M. Bond returned from hospital to duty with D Coy.	R.J.
	10.30 am	C.O visited trenches	R.J.
9th		Situation normal. Sick wastage nil.	R.J.
	10.30 am	Major C. S. Heathcote D.S.O left Battn to take over command of 1/4 Lincolns.	R.J.
	10.5 am	Message sent to trenches to take cover for a bombardment.	R.J.
			R.J.
	10.25 am	All ready.	R.J.
		H.Q moved to dugouts. Telephones working well	R.J.
		Casualties other ranks wounded 3.	R.J.
10th		Situation normal. Sick wastage one. diarrhoea	R.J.
		Casualties other ranks killed 2. wounded one	R.J.
	2.30 pm	C.O and Bde Major visited trenches	R.J.

(73989) W4141—463. 400,000. 9/14. H.&J.Ltd. Forms/C. 2118/10.

Instructions regarding War Diaries and Intelligence Summaries are contained in F. S. Regs., Part II. and the Staff Manual respectively. Title pages will be prepared in manuscript.

WAR DIARY

or

~~INTELLIGENCE SUMMARY.~~

(Erase heading not required.)

Army Form C. 2118.

3/

Hour, Date, Place	Summary of Events and Information	Remarks and references to Appendices
Sept 10th Trenches	Artillery tested.	
	18th Battery replied in 45 seconds	L.G.T.
	22nd " " " 15 "	
11th	Situation normal.	L.G.T.
	Sick wastage one. Casualties other ranks wounded 1	L.G.T.
	Lieut. W. T. Key missing. He went out at night in front of the wire and no trace could be found of him.	L.G.T.
	Subsidiary line shelled from 9.45 am – 12.15 pm	L.G.T.
	Howitzer Battery retaliated.	L.G.T.
	Relieved by 2nd East Lancs	L.G.T.
9.25pm	Relief complete	L.G.T.
12th Scherpenberg.	Major Mallinson D.S.O. returned and Capt Tewson proceeded on leave.	L.G.T.
12th–17th	Battalion resting	L.G.T.
14th	Battalion inspected by Sir Herbert Plumer K.C.B. Cmdg 2nd Army. Report attached.	L.G.T.
15th	Draft of 30 other ranks joined. Report attached.	L.G.T.

(73989) W4141—463. 400,000. 9/14. H.&J.Ltd. Forms/C. 2118/10.

Instructions regarding War Diaries and Intelligence Summaries are contained in F. S. Regs., Part II. and the Staff Manual respectively. Title pages will be prepared in manuscript.

WAR DIARY

or

~~INTELLIGENCE SUMMARY~~.

(Erase heading not required.)

Army Form C. 2118.

4

Hour, Date, Place		Summary of Events and Information	Remarks and references to Appendices
Sept 17th	Trenches	Battn relieved 2nd East Yorks in the trenches	SCP
	9.15pm	Relief complete	SCP
18th		Situation normal. Sick wastage O.R. 3.	SCP
		Casualties other ranks killed 2.	SCP
	10 am	C.O. visited trenches	SCP
19th		Situation normal. Sick wastage. O.R. 3.	SCP
		Casualties O.R. wounded 3.	SCP
		Capt Tewson returned from leave	SCP
		Officers of 22nd Canadian Infantry reconnoitred trenches. C.O. came to Battn H.Q.	SCP
	11 pm	2nd in Command visited trenches.	SCP
20th		Situation normal. Sick wastage other ranks 3	SCP
		Casualties nil	SCP
		1½ Coys 22nd Canadians relieved 1½ Coys R.W.F. in the trenches. M.G.s of 22nd were brought up but not mounted.	SCP
	11 pm	Relief complete.	SCP
	11.15pm	2nd in Command, O.C. and 2nd in Command 22nd Canadians visited trenches.	SCP

(73989) W4141—463. 400,000. 9/14. H.&J.Ltd. Forms/C. 2118/10.

Army Form C. 2118.

Instructions regarding War Diaries and Intelligence Summaries are contained in F. S. Regs., Part II. and the Staff Manual respectively. Title pages will be prepared in manuscript.

WAR DIARY
or
~~INTELLIGENCE~~ SUMMARY.
(Erase heading not required.)

Hour, Date, Place	Summary of Events and Information	Remarks and references to Appendices
Sept 21. Trenches	Situation normal. Sick wastage nil. Casualties KOYLI nil. 22nd Canadians O.R. wounded one.	S.P.
3pm	2nd in Command 22nd Canadians and Adjutant KOYLI visited trenches.	S.P.
	Officers 26th Canadians reconnoitred trenches.	S.P.
	C.O and Adjutant at Batt. H.Q.	S.P.
	2 M.Gs KOYLI withdrawn and 22nd Canadians mounted their guns.	S.P.
10.30pm	2nd in Command visited trenches.	S.P.
22nd	Situation normal. Sick wastage nil. Casualties KOYLI O.R. wounded 2. Canadians nil.	S.P.
10.30 am	C.O KOYLI and C.O and Adjutant 26th Canadians visited trenches	S.P.
3pm	Remaining 2 M.Gs of KOYLI withdrawn.	S.P.
4pm	½ Coy KOYLI relieved by ½ Coy 22nd Canadians	S.P.
8.50pm	Relief completed of remaining Coy KOYLI in the trenches and of reserve Coy KOYLI	S.P.
	Battalion bivouacked near SCHERPENBERG for the night.	S.P.
	Bde pioneers, 8 Bde miners, Bde section, Bde postman, [illegible] and [illegible] rejoined Battn.	S.P.

(73989) W4141—463. 400,000. 9/14. H.&J.Ltd. Forms/C. 2118/10.

7/6.

Army Form C. 2118.

WAR DIARY
or
~~INTELLIGENCE SUMMARY.~~

(*Erase heading not required.*)

Instructions regarding War Diaries and Intelligence Summaries are contained in F. S. Regs., Part II. and the Staff Manual respectively. Title pages will be prepared in manuscript.

Hour, Date, Place	Summary of Events and Information	Remarks and references to Appendices
Sept 22	Lieut Kemble proceeded on leave.	T.S.
23.	Bde marched to billets at OUTTERSTEENE	T.S.
9 a.m	Battn left SCHERPENBERG at 9 a m and marched via LOCRE and BAILLEUL, arrived in billets at 12.30	
12.30 pm	pm. Sir Charles Fergusson watched Bde pass in BAILLEUL. Battalion ordered to be in readiness to move at an hours notice	T.S.
24. OUTTERSTEENE 9.30 am	Battalion route march	T.S.
5 pm.	Physical drill.	T.S.
25. 6.30 am	Physical drill.	T.S.
9.30 am	Battalion fell in on alarm post ready for entrainment. G.O.C. 83rd Bde inspected the Battn	T.S.
10 a.m	Afterwards route march	T.S.
	Attached message received	T.S.
5.50 pm	S.C. 494 attached received.	T.S.
6.15 pm	S.C. 497 " " and all blankets stored	T.S.
7 pm	S.C. 499 " "	T.S.
7.15 pm	B.M.A. 560 received.	T.S.

87

Instructions regarding War Diaries and Intelligence Summaries are contained in F. S. Regs., Part II. and the Staff Manual respectively. Title pages will be prepared in manuscript.

WAR DIARY
or
~~INTELLIGENCE~~ SUMMARY.

(*Erase heading not required.*)

Army Form C. 2118.

Hour, Date, Place		Summary of Events and Information	Remarks and references to Appendices
Sept 26th OUTTERSTEEN.	6 a.m	Left OUTTERSTEEN 6 a.m and marched to ROBECQ via MERVILLE	
	11.15 a.m	Arrived ROBECQ.	
	2 p.m	Left Robecq and marched towards BETHUNE. after marching about 1½ miles, Column was halted, and then returned to ROBECQ.	
		Battn billeted in ROBECQ for the night.	
27th ROBECQ.	1 p.m.	Battalion embussed.	
	3.30 p.m	Reached NOYELLES LES VERMELLES and bivouacked for the night.	
		Co, Adjutant and Company Commanders went up to 2nd Bde H.Q to reconnoitre trenches. On arrival at Bde H.Q found relief was cancelled.	
28th NOYELLES LES VERMELLES.	2 p.m	Occupied reserve trenches on VERMELLES road as a bombardment was expected.	
	5.30 p.m	Returned to Bivouacs.	
29th	10 a.m	Battn ordered to be ready to move at Short notice	
	10.15 a.m	Battn moved.	

8

Army Form C. 2118.

Instructions regarding War Diaries and Intelligence Summaries are contained in F. S. Regs., Part II. and the Staff Manual respectively. Title pages will be prepared in manuscript.

WAR DIARY
or
~~INTELLIGENCE SUMMARY.~~

(Erase heading not required.)

Hour, Date, Place	Summary of Events and Information	Remarks and references to Appendices
Sept 29 Trenches	B and D Companies under Major Mallinson D.S.O occupied Sussex Trench.	B.P.
	HQ and remainder of Battn in Lancashire Lines	B.P.
2.15 pm	B and D moved and came under orders of 85th Bde. D Coy in firing line in "BIG WILLIE", B in support.	B.P.
5 pm	Remainder of Battn moved up in to Reserve trench and came under orders of 85th Bde	B.P.
30th	Casualties. 2Lt A. H. Robson 3rd D.L.I attached 1st KOYLI wounded. 2Lt L. G. Welch 1st KOYLI sick to hospital.	B.P.
	Other ranks killed 2 wounded 8.	B.P.
	2Lt F. N. Brooke joined 83rd Bde as Bde Bomb Officer.	B.P.
4 pm	Battn (except D Coy) relieved and proceeded to old English front line trenches N of HULLOCH Road, arriving there at 2.15 a.m on 1st Oct.	B.P.

(73989) W4141—463. 400,000. 9/14. H.&J.Ltd. Forms/C. 2118/10.

Information concerning men of Draft which joined 1st K.O.Y.L.I. 15th Sept. 1915

3256. Acting Sgt. Ruggin W. killed 8 Nov. 1914. Rejoined 21. Left England 20-7-15.

9608 Corpl. Rickhurst B. rejoined on recovering from wound received in April 1915

20853 L/C Corp. Widdowson C. rejoined on recovering from wound received in August 1915.

20539 Pte Mason H. rejoined on recovering from wound received in August 1915.

20331 Pte Lee C. rejoined on recovering from wound received in August 1915

20264 Pte Hughes A. rejoined on recovering from wound received in July 1915

Information re Draft 15-7-15 cont: (8)

25648 Pte G. Baker rejoined on recovery from wound received in August 1915.

10493 Pte Mason G. rejoined on recovering from wound received in August 1915

28211 Pte Willoughby G. rejoined, having been in Hospital for 7 weeks.

21967 Pte Smith, O. rejoined, having been in Hospital for 6 weeks, ~~[illegible]~~ subject to "fits".

10308 Pte Carr. R. rejoined. having left the Bn in Feb. 15 sick.

21364 Pte Gray. W. rejoined, having been in Hospital for 12 weeks.

3118 Pte Brannon D. rejoined. Originally joined the Bn on the 22 July 1915, was sent to the Base for permanent duty, having been reported by the A.D.M.S. 28th Div to be "unfit" for duty in the trenches owing to a deformed right arm the result of an old fracture.

Forwarded to the Base on the 13-8-15

Information re Drafts 5-9-15 Cont'd (4)

22026 Pte [illegible] 3rd Bn. Enlisted 10-3-15. Age 19. Came out to the Country 2-9-15.

2205[illegible] Pte [illegible] 3rd Bn. Enlisted 12-3-15. Age 22. Came out to the Country 2-9-15.

22026 Pte Nicholson J. 3rd Bn. Enlisted 6-2-15. Age 34. Came out to the Country 2-9-15

22619 Rflp. Hornby J. 3rd Bn. Enlisted 7-5-15. Age 20 [illegible]. Came out to the Country 2-9-15

22620 Pte Sparkes T. 3rd Bn. Enlisted 23-3-15. Age 36. Came out to the Country 2-9-15

2043 Sgt Swallow A. Enlisted 3-11-14 in 11th Bn. Sent to 3rd Bn in Feb. 1915 in consequence of displaced cartilage of the knee. Now recovered. Age 28. Came out to the Country 2-9-15

Information re Draft. 15-9-15 Cont: (3)

19244 Pte. Kastelow E. rejoined. Originally joined the Battalion on the 29th July 1915. Was sent to the Base for permanent duty having been reported by the A.D.M.S. 28th Division to be unfit for duty in the Trenches owing to chronic inflammation of left knee joint. Proceeded to the Base on the 13-8-15.

22131 Pte. Hunter G. from 3rd Bn. Enlisted 16-3-15. Age 35. Came out to the Country on the 3-9-15

21894 Pte. Doughty. W. 3rd Bn. Enlisted 1-3-15. Age 28. Came out to the Country in June. Has been in Hospital at the Base for 7 weeks with Syphilis.

22196 Pte. Edwards J.W. 3rd Bn. Enlisted 23-3-15. Age 28. Came out to the Country on the 3-9-15

22499 Pte. Lee W. 3rd Bn. Enlisted 26-4-15. Age 30. Came out to the Country on the 3-9-15

Information re Draft. 15-9-15 [illegible] (5)

19856 Pte [illegible] H. Enlisted 11-11-14 in the 11th Bn. Sent to 3rd Bn. in Feb. '15 fit for home service only. Rheumatism in legs & feet. Age 46. Came out to the Country 3-9-15.

14897 Pte Rogers B. Enlisted 10-11-14 in the 11th Bn. Sent to 3rd Bn. in February 15. Fit for home service only. Defective teeth. Reports he has received no treatment. Age 36. Came out to the Country 3-9-15

23186 L/Cp. A Royston. Enlisted 8-9-14 in the 5th D. Gds. Transferred to 3rd Bn June 15. Age 21. Came out to the Country 3-9-15

23561 Pte J. Williams Enlisted 3-9-14 in the 15th Hussars, Transferred to 3rd Bn. June 1915. Age 35. Came out to the Country 3-9-15.

23560 Pte Watson H. Enlisted 5-9-14 in the 15th Hussars. Transferred to 3rd Bn June 1915. Age 30. Came out to the Country 3-9-15.

(6)

Information re Draft 15-9-15 [illegible]

22452 J. Hurley H.J. [illegible]

8-9-14 [illegible] The 5th D. Bn. [illegible]

to 2nd Rein. June 1915. Age 20.

Commenced to the Country 3-7-15

"C" Form (Original). Army Form C. 2123.

MESSAGES AND SIGNALS. No. of Message

Prefix ___ Code ___ Words ___	Received	Sent, or sent out	Office Stamp.
£ s. d. Charges to collect	From ___ By ___	At ___ m.	
Service Instructions. [illegible]		To ___ By ___	

Handed in at ___ Office ___ m. Received ___ m.

TO [illegible]

*Sender's Number	Day of Month	In reply to Number	AAA
SC 491	25,		

1st	Army	wire	8.40 a.m.	all
Divisions	South	of	BETHUNE	LA
BASSEE	Road	have	all	reached
the	front line	trenches	on	[illegible]
[illegible]	[illegible]	move	[illegible]	aaa
Between	LA	BASSEE	Road	and
Canal	[illegible]	[illegible]	[illegible]	checked
aaa	following	places	reported	to
be	occupied	by	our	troops
including	[illegible]	[illegible]	LOOS	PYLONS
Cemetery	west	of	LOOS	and
FOSSE	No. 8	aaa	2 Bdes	15th Div
[illegible]	[illegible]	[illegible]	towards	and
[illegible]	of	LOOS	aaa	1st Div
checked	temporarily	by	gas	7th
and	9th	Div	reported	progressing

FROM 82nd Bde

PLACE & TIME 11.50 am

*This line should be erased if not required.

(25555). M.R.Co.,Ltd. Wt.W1789/1402. 70,000 Pads—6/15. Forms/C.2123.

"C" Form (Original). Army Form C. 2123.

MESSAGES AND SIGNALS.

No. of Message..........

Prefix.......... Code.......... Words..........

£ s. d.

Charges to collect

Received From ZHC By [illegible]

Sent, or sent out At..........m. To.......... By..........

Office Stamp. [illegible] 25/9/15

Service Instructions. ZHC

Handed in at.......... Office..........m. Received..........m.

TO All Units

*Sender's Number	Day of Month	In reply to Number	AAA
FC 492	25		

1st	Army	reports	10 a.m	that
Loos	is in	our	hands	and
that	our	infantry	are	advancing
on	Hill 70	AAA	1st Div	is
advancing	on	HULLUCH	and	has
captured	2 guns	AAA	7th Div	is
between	HULLUCH	and	DAISNES	AAA
9th Div	have	taken	FOSSE	8 after
and	is	advancing	on	DAISNES
AAA	Right	of	2nd Div	is
held	up	about	LES	BRIQUES
AAA	Indians	have	reported	capture
of	MOULIN	DU	PIETRE	and
142	prisoners	AAA	14th Div	report
9 42	a.m	that	reached	line
J 12	d.1.6	I 20.b.4	J 12 a.0.2	AAA

FROM

PLACE & TIME

*This line should be erased if not required.

(25555). M.R.Co.,Ltd. Wt.W1789/1402. 70,000 Pads—6/15. Forms/C.2123.

"C" Form (Duplicate). Army Form C. 2123.

MESSAGES AND SIGNALS.

No. of Message..........

	Charges to Pay. £ s. d.	Office Stamp.
Service Instructions. 2 H C		

Handed in at.......... Office.......... m. Received.......... m.

TO [illegible]

Sender's Number	Day of Month	In reply to Number	AAA
	25		

1st	Army	reports	at 9 a.m.	aaa
4th	Corps	have	crossed	German
first	line	trenches	on the	approach
front	of	LENS	to	LA
BASSE	Canal	aaa	1st Div	advance
is	slow	owing	to	gas
hanging	front	of	it	aaa
1st	Corps	attack	on	GIVENCHY
successful	aaa	MEERUT	DIV	further
on	[illegible]	have	taken	about
120	prisoners	aaa	Right	of
8th Div	3rd	Corps	N.E.	of
the	AUBERS	Ridge	has	reached
German	2nd	line	trenches	while
left	is	in	front	line
trenches				

FROM 23rd Bde
PLACE & TIME 11.20 a.m.

(25555). M.R.Co.,Ltd. Wt. W1789/1402. 70,000 Pads—6/15. Forms/C.2123.

"A" Form. Army Form C. 2121.

MESSAGES AND SIGNALS.

No. of Message

Prefix / Code m.	Words	Charge	This message is on a/c of:	Recd. at m.
Office of Origin and Service Instructions: Copy	Sent At m. To By		Service. (Signature of "Franking Officer.")	Date From By

TO: O.C. 1st [illegible]

* Sender's Number	Day of Month	In reply to Number	AAA
	3rd		

Sgt	Brady	and	party	did
excellent	work	last	night	on
Saturday	line	under	difficult	and
unfavourable		conditions		

From: O.C. 1st [illegible] Coy R.E.

Place

Time: 6 p.m.

The above may be forwarded as now corrected.

Censor.

(Z)

Signature of Addressor or person authorised to telegraph in his name.

* This line should be erased if not required.

(5431) S. & Co. Ltd. W 14142/641. 90,000. 4/15. Forms C 2121/10.

"C" Form (Duplicate). Army Form C. 2123.

MESSAGES AND SIGNALS.

No. of Message.................

	Charges to Pay. £ s. d.	Office Stamp.
Service Instructions.		

Handed in at .... Office .... m. Received .... m.

TO

Sender's Number	Day of Month	In reply to Number	AAA

They	were	heavily	[illegible]	attacked
and	driven	back	to	original
front	[illegible]	[illegible]	line	together
with	[illegible]	7.12 a.m.	AAA	3rd Div
at	11.5	a.m.	2 officers	and
100	other	ranks	[illegible]	[illegible]
men	have	been	captured	AAA
[illegible]	[illegible]	11.15 a.m.	report	Germans
[illegible]	[illegible]	have	been	captured
French	report	all	[illegible]	were
Champagne	[illegible]	first	line	has
been	taken	on	the	whole
front	[illegible]	advance	progressing	
normally				

FROM
PLACE & TIME 83rd Bde
2.30 pm

(25555). M.R.Co ,Ltd. Wt.W1789/1402. 70,000 Pads—6/15. Forms/C.2123.

28th.Division wire begins:-

3rd.Divn.reports having captured about 50 prisoners of 172nd.Regt. in J.19a.and J.13c.

1st.Gordons reported in Front Line Trenches about I. I.18.D.8.4.

4th.Gordons on their right have taken their three lines of G rman Trenches and are in touch with Royal Scots in German First line trenches further South.

14th.Divn.report having captured front line trenches I.12a.8.5.

10.20.am. 25-9-15.

"C" Form (Duplicate). Army Form C. 2123.

MESSAGES AND SIGNALS. No. of Message

Service Instructions.	Charges to Pay. £ s. d.	Office Stamp.
[illegible]		

Handded in at .... Office .... m. Received .... m.

TO [illegible]

Sender's Number	Day of Month	In reply to Number	AAA
G.494	25		

You	will	hold	yourself	in
readiness	to	proceed	by	train
at	2	hours	notice	
if	ordered			

FROM PLACE & TIME: 83rd Bde
5 50 pm

(25555). M.R.Co.,Ltd. Wt.W1789/1402. 70,000 Pads—6/15. Forms/C.2123.

"C" Form (Original). Army Form C. 2123.

MESSAGES AND SIGNALS. No. of Message..........

Prefix......Code......Words......	Received	Sent, or sent out	Office Stamp.
£ s. d. Charges to collect	From...... By......	At......m. To...... By......	
Service Instructions. Z H C			

Handed in at...... Office......m. Received......m.

TO All units

*Sender's Number	Day of Month	In reply to Number	AAA
SC 497	25		

Blankets	to	School	2 pm	

FROM 83rd Bde
PLACE & TIME 6.15 pm

*This line should be erased if not required.

(25555). M.R.Co.,Ltd. Wt.W1789/1402. 70,000 Pads—6/15. Forms/C.2123.

"C" Form (...cate). Army Form C. 2123.

MESSAGES AND SIGNALS. No. of Message

Service Instructions. 2 HC	Charges to Pay. £ s. d.	Office Stamp.

Handed in at Office m. Received m.

TO All units

Sender's Number	Day of Month	In reply to Number	AAA
S C 499	25th		

By	main	route	do	not
return	SAA			

FROM 83rd Bde

PLACE & TIME 7 pm

(25555). M.R.Co.,Ltd. Wt.W1739/1402. 70,000 Pads—6/15. Forms/C.2123.

"A" Form.

Army Form C. 2121.

MESSAGES AND SIGNALS.

No. of Message

...m.	Words.	Charge.	This message is on a/c of:	Recd. at ...m.
...ce Instructions.	Sent		... Service.	Date
	At ...m.			From
	To			By
	By		(Signature of "Franking Officer.")	

1/ K.O.Y.L.I.

Sender's Number	Day of Month	In reply to Number	AAA
	29th		

Proceed with remainder of 1st K.O.Y.L.I. to 85th Brigade.

From 83rd Bde

Place

Time 6 p.m.

The above may be forwarded as now corrected. (Z) sd. R.S. Follett.

Censor. Signature of Addressor or person authorised to telegraph in his name

* This line should be erased if not required.

(473). M.R.Co.,Ltd. Wt.W4843/541. 50,000. 9/14. Forms C2121/10.

Copy

1ST KING'S OWN YORKSHIRE LIGHT INFANTRY

sd. C. R. Ingham Brooke, Lt-Col.

Field State 14·9·15

Distribution.	Officers	W.O's	Sergts	Cpls.	Buglers	Ptes.	Total	Remarks
A Coy	4	1	7	6	–	168	182	
B Coy	3	–	11	7	–	150	168	
C Coy	3	1	8	8	–	158	170	
D Coy	3	1	8	6	–	158	173	
Pioneers	–	–	1	–	–	10	11	
Signallers	–	–	–	1	–	19	20	
Machine Gns.	1	–	3	1	–	24	28	
Stretcher Brs.	1	–	–	–	–	17	17	
Hd. Qrs.	4	1	–	–	–	–	1	
	21	4	38	29	–	699	770	

Parade State on 14·9·15 when the Battalion was inspected by Gen. Sir H. Plumer, K.C.B.

Comdg 2nd Army.

Copy

B.M.A. 560.

Officer Commanding

K.O.Y.L.I.

1. Reference S.C 494, the move, if ordered, will now probably take place by train; 2nd Kings Own, 1st York & Lancs. & 5th Kings Own from Bailleul. 1st K.O.Y.L.I. & 2nd E. Yorks from Strazeele. No 1st Line Transport will be entrained, except as stated in para. 2.

2. All machine guns of the Bde with their limbers, horses, etc, will entrain at Bailleul.

3. 50 rds. extra per man will be carried.

Acknowledge.

83rd Bde. H.Q.
25/9/15.

sd. R. S. Follett
Major,
Brigade Major
83rd Bde.

83rd Bde.
28th Div.

WAR DIARY

Moved with Division to Salonika in November.

1st K. O. Y. L. I.

O C T O B E R

1 9 1 5.

Instructions regarding War Diaries and Intelligence Summaries are contained in F. S. Regs., Part II. and the Staff Manual respectively. Title pages will be prepared in manuscript.

WAR DIARY
or
INTELLIGENCE ~~SUMMARY~~.
(*Erase heading not required.*)

Army Form C. 2118.

Hour, Date, Place		Summary of Events and Information	Remarks and references to Appendices
Oct. 1st	Trenches. 5.45 a.m	Battn ordered to move up and occupy old German front line trenches.	S.a.P.
	10.3.a.m	D Coy relieved and proceeded to Lancashire Lines	S.a.P.
		Casualties Lt. T. L. Beattie killed. other ranks killed 5 wounded 31.	S.a.P.
		Right of Battn rested on HULLUCH-VERMELLES road. Left just north of BRESLAU Avenue.	S.a.P.
		Battn relieved by 2nd H.L.I. and proceeded to billets at ANNEQUIN.	S.a.P.
2nd	ANNEQUIN	In billets at ANNEQUIN.	S.a.P.
3rd	6.30 am	Battn ordered to be ready to move at very short notice.	S.a.P.
	7 a.m	C.O. went with Brigadier to 28th Div HdQ	S.a.P.
	9 a.m	Battn marched to CLARKS KEEP VERMELLES	S.a.P.
	10.30 am	Battn marched to trenches and relieved 6th Welch. Battn in firing line. one Company 2nd Kings Own in support.	S.a.P.
	6.10 pm	Relief complete	S.a.P.

(73989) W4141—463. 400,000. 9/14. H.&J.Ltd. Forms/C. 2118/10.

Instructions regarding War Diaries and Intelligence Summaries are contained in F. S. Regs., Part II. and the Staff Manual respectively. Title pages will be prepared in manuscript.

WAR DIARY
or
~~INTELLIGENCE SUMMARY.~~
(*Erase heading not required.*)

Army Form C. 2118.

2

Hour, Date, Place		Summary of Events and Information	Remarks and references to Appendices
Oct 3rd	Trenches. 11pm	C.O and Major Mallinson D.S.O went to Bde H.Q.	R.P.
4th		A and D Coys ordered to attack HOHENZOLLERN Redoubt. (See B.M. 644) attached.	R.P.
	4.45am	A and D attacked and were met with very heavy machine gun and rifle fire. There was no artillery bombardment. The distance to the German line was about 200 yards and the men got half way across. By then they were practically wiped out.	R.P. // See Ops. orders 4/83 Bde – perhaps he means the enemy did not – bombard?
		Casualties 2/Lt. A. H. Martindale 1st KOYLI killed. 2/Lt. C. L. Pearn " wounded. Lt. F. W. Graham 4th D.L.I. att. 1st KOYLI missing 2/Lt. P. J. C. Simpson 3rd KOYLI " " " Other ranks killed 10. wounded 65. missing 101. There is no doubt that most of the missing were killed. A few wounded were got in during the night 4/5th	R.P.

(73989) W4141—463. 400,000. 9/14. H.&J.Ltd. Forms/C. 2118/10.

Instructions regarding War Diaries and Intelligence Summaries are contained in F. S. Regs., Part II. and the Staff Manual respectively. Title pages will be prepared in manuscript.

WAR DIARY
or
~~INTELLIGENCE SUMMARY~~.
(Erase heading not required.)

Army Form C. 2118.

183

Hour, Date, Place		Summary of Events and Information	Remarks and references to Appendices
Oct. 5th	Trenches	Battn relieved by 1st Coldstream Guards	[initials]
		Casualties killed one. wounded 2.	
	10.30 pm	Relief complete.	[initials]
		Battn marched to billets at ANNEQUIN.	
		Draft of Sec Buglers and 97 O.R. joined.	
6th	12 noon	Battn marched by BEUVRY – BETHUNE – OBLINGHEM to	[initials]
		Billets near BONNEHEM arriving at 5.10 pm	[initials]
7th	BONNEHEM.	Battn in billets.	[initials]
	11 am	Draft of 51 other ranks joined	
8th	6.30 am	6.30 a.m physical drill	[initials]
	9 am	Platoon drill.	[initials]
	12 noon	Musketry.	[initials]
	2.30 pm	Company drill	[initials]
		Instruction of Grenadiers.	
9th	6.30 am	Physical training	[initials]
	9 a.m	Company parades.	[initials]
	2.30 pm	practice in trench warfare. Training of Grenadiers	

Army Form C. 2118.

Instructions regarding War Diaries and Intelligence Summaries are contained in F. S. Regs., Part II. and the Staff Manual respectively. Title pages will be prepared in manuscript.

WAR DIARY
or
~~INTELLIGENCE~~ SUMMARY.
(Erase heading not required.)

Hour, Date, Place	Summary of Events and Information	Remarks and references to Appendices
Oct 10. GONNEHEM	Church parades for all denominations.	[illegible]
	2Lt. W. S. Howard KOYLI joined from 8th Entrenching Battn and was posted to A Coy.	[illegible]
13th 9 am	Brigade inspected by G.O.C. 28th Division	
	2Lts G. M. Plaskitt and A. T. Jarvis, 10th and 12th Essex Regt joined and were posted to A and D Coys. Draft of 70 O.R. joined.	[illegible]
14th 9 am	Battn Route March.	[illegible]
	Draft of 12 O.R. joined.	[illegible]
2.30 pm	Musketry.	
	Capt and Quartermaster J. C. Bramer and 2Lt A. E. Gedsson proceeded on leave. Lt Robinson wounded Bomb accident.	[illegible]
15th 9 a.m	Physical training.	[illegible]
9.30 a.m	G.O.C. 83rd Bde inspected drafts which arrived on 5th, 7th, 13th, 14th.	[illegible]
1.30 pm	Attached B.M. 730 Received.	[illegible]
4 pm	Battn marched via CHOCQUES - BETHUNE to billets at LE QUESNOY.	[illegible]
8 pm	Arrived in billets.	[illegible]

(73989) W4141—463. 400,000. 9/14. H.&J.Ltd. Forms/C. 2118/10.

Instructions regarding War Diaries and Intelligence Summaries are contained in F. S. Regs., Part II. and the Staff Manual respectively. Title pages will be prepared in manuscript.

WAR DIARY
or
~~INTELLIGENCE SUMMARY.~~
(Erase heading not required.)

Army Form C. 2118.

5

Hour, Date, Place		Summary of Events and Information	Remarks and references to Appendices
Oct 16.	LE QUESNOY. 10.15 am	Commanding officer and Company Commanders went up to reconnoitre trenches.	SGF
	11 a.m	2Lt. J. N. Plaskitt 10th Essex att'd 1st Kings wounded himself whilst cleaning his revolver	SGF
17th	9 a.m	Batt'n marched from LE QUESNOY and relieved 2nd Queens in the trenches	SGF
	12.45 pm	Relief complete.	SGF
	7 pm	Lt. A. E. Kemble wounded.	SGF
18th	Trenches	Situation normal. Casualties other ranks wounded 8.	SGF
19th	10 am	G.O.C. 28th Division visited trenches.	SGF
		Casualties other ranks wounded 2.	SGF
20th	9.45 am	G.O.C 1st Corps visited trenches.	SGF
21st		Batt'n relieved by 5th Kings and 2nd South Staffords	SGF
	12.30 pm	Relief complete. After relief Batt'n marched to Billets at CENSE LA VALLÉE.	SGF
		No 5516 C.S.M. J. Lawn awarded a clasp to his D.C.M.	SGF
22nd	CENSE LA VALLÉE	Batt'n in Billets	SGF

Instructions regarding War Diaries and Intelligence Summaries are contained in F. S. Regs., Part II. and the Staff Manual respectively. Title pages will be prepared in manuscript.

WAR DIARY

or

~~INTELLIGENCE SUMMARY.~~

(*Erase heading not required.*)

Army Form C. 2118.

6

Hour, Date, Place		Summary of Events and Information	Remarks and references to Appendices
Oct 23rd	6.30 am	Battn entrained at FOUQUEREUIL and proceeded to MARSEILLES.	TaT
25th	10.30 a.m	Arrived at MARSEILLES and embarked on S.S. KYARA, with 83rd Bde H.Q and 18 Officers 2nd Kings Own Regt.	TaT
31st	2.20 pm	Arrived at ALEXANDRIA.	TaT

(73989) W4141—463. 400,000. 9/14. H.&J.Ltd. Forms/C. 2118/10.

"A" Form. Army Form C. 2121

MESSAGES AND SIGNALS.

No. of Message

Prefix ... Code ... m.	Words	Charge	This message is on a/c of:	Recd. at ... m.
Office of Origin and Service Instructions	Sent		... Service.	Date
Corps	At ... m.			From
	To			By
	By		(Signature of "Franking Officer.")	

TO { 1st Koyli.

Sender's Number	Day of Month	In reply to Number	AAA
* BM 622	3rd		

Battn	will	march	off	at
9	a.m.	to	CLARKS	KEEP
VERMELLES		where	Brigade	will
meet	you	with	your	Guide
officer	aaa			

From 83rd Bde

Place

Time 8.10 am

The above may be forwarded as now corrected. ... Censor.

(Z) Sd. R. S. Follett Major

Signature of Addressor or person authorised to telegraph in his name.

* This line should be erased if not required.

(15191) S. & Co. Ltd. W 14142/641. 90,000. 4/15. Forms C 2121/10.

Copy

"A" Form.

Army Form C. 2121.

MESSAGES AND SIGNALS.

No. of Message

Prefix Code m.	Words	Charge	This message is on a/c of:	Recd. at m.
Office of Origin and Service Instructions	Sent		Service.	Date
	At m.			From
	To			
	By		(Signature of "Franking Officer.")	By

TO 1st K.O.Y.L.I.

Sender's Number	Day of Month	In reply to Number	AAA
* B.M. 613	1st		

Your Battalion will move to the 1st Line of old German Trenches with its right on Vermelles – Hulloch Rd. AAA. The Battalion should be extended to cover communication Trenches as far as Breslau Avenue AAA. Acknowledge & inform this office when you move AAA Troops of 21st Brigade are in front of you.

From 88th Bde.

Place

Time 4.45 a.m.

The above may be forwarded as now corrected.

Censor.

(Z) sd R. S. Hollett.

Signature of Addressor or person authorised to telegraph in his name.

* This line should be erased if not required.

(15491) S. & Co. Ltd. W 14142/611. 90,000. 1/15. Forms C 2121/10.

"C" Form (Triplicate). Army Form C. 2123 A.

MESSAGES AND SIGNALS. No. of Message..................

Prm · E G pm 2 H. C Service Instructions	Charges to Pay £ s. d. 1/10/15.	Office Stamp. 7.0 pm 2 H C JSB

Handed in at the......................................Office, at..............................m. Received here at..............................m.

TO 1/ K. O. Y. L. I. 6th King Own

Sender's Number	Day of Month.	In reply to Number.	AAA
B M B 41	1st		

Brigade will be relieved tonight aaa Units will hand over trenches to Battalions of relieving Brigade as already arranged except 1/K.O.Y.L.I who will receive instructions through 21/Bde aaa Guides to conduct all units to billeting area will be at Bde Hqrs aaa Machine gun limbers will be at Bde Hqrs aaa

FROM 83rd Infantry Bde

PLACE

TIME

GALE & POLDEN, LTD. PRINTERS, ALDERSHOT.
(69,017). Wt. 7981—443. 40,000 Pads. 4/13. W.

Extract from the London Gazette
4th Oct.

Soms. L.I.
To be temp. Lieut Col.
Major C.R.I. Brooke
from Dec 1st 1914 to May 8,
and from Aug. 26th
Major W. Swans (since died of wounds)
from Sept 17 1914 to Nov 29. 1914
Major C.E. Heathcote relinq. temp.
rank of Lieut. Col August 26.

"C" Form. Army Form C. 2121.

MESSAGES AND SIGNALS.

No. of Message ....

Prefix ...... Code ...... m.	Words	Charge	This message is on a/c of:	Recd. at ...... m.
Office of Origin and Service Instructions	Sent		.... Service.	Date
Copy	At ...... m.			From
	To			
	By		(Signature of "Franking Officer.")	By

TO			
2nd	East	Yorks	
1/ KOYLI			

Sender's Number	Day of Month	In reply to Number	AAA
* BM 644	4		

At	4.45	a.m	4th Oct	15
2nd East	Yorks	Regt	and	2 Coys
1st KOYLI	will	one Coy	2nd	Kings
Own	Regt	attached	will	assault
HOHEN	ZOLLERN	REDO	UBT	aaa
First	objective	western	face	of
redoubt	Second	objective	THE	CHORD
aaa	At	4.15	a.m	Artillery
will	bombard	line	heavily	until
4.45	a.m	when	they	will
lift	on	to	enemy's	communication
trenches	aaa	when	the	first
bombardment		commences	the	first
and	second	line	of	platoons
will	get	over	the	parapet
advance	towards	the	enemy	parapet
and	lie	down	aaa	absolute

From			
Place			
Time			

The above may be forwarded as now corrected. .... Censor.	(Z) .... Signature of Addressor or person authorised to telegraph in his name.

* This line should be erased if not required.

(15491) S. & Co. Ltd. W 14142/611. 90,000. 1/15. Forms C 2121/10.

"A" Form. Army Form C. 2121.

MESSAGES AND SIGNALS.

No. of Message ....

Prefix ...... Code ...... m.	Words	Charge	This message is on a/c of:	Recd. at ...... m.
Office of Origin and Service Instructions	*Sent		...... Service.	Date ......
	At ...... m.			From ......
	To			
	By		(Signature of "Franking Officer.")	By

TO

Sender's Number *	Day of Month	In reply to Number	AAA

Silence	will	be	maintained	until
the	enemy	trench	is	reached
AAA	The	assault	of	the
CHORD	will	be	undertaken	
without	delay	once	the	western
face	has	been	gained	AAA
All	communication		trenches	leading
from	captured	works	towards	the
enemy	will	be	filled	in
and	blocked	AAA	Two	sections
R. E.	will	follow	behind	the
last	platoons	and	dig	communication
trenches	back	from	captured	works
to	old	British	line	AAA
Signal	officer	85th	Bde	will
arrange	to	place	a	telephone
on	western	face	of	REDOUBT

From			
Place			
Time			

The above may be forwarded as now corrected. ...... Censor.	(Z) ...... Signature of Addressor or person authorised to telegraph in his name.

* This line should be erased if not required.

(15491) S. & Co. Ltd. W 14142 641. 30 000. 1 15. Forms C 2121/10.

"A" Form. Army Form C. 2121.

MESSAGES AND SIGNALS.

No. of Message ______

Prefix ___ Code ___ m. Office of Origin and Service Instructions. C 67	Words	Charge	This message is on a/c of: ______ Service. (Signature of "Franking Officer.")	Recd. at ______ m.
	Sent At ______ m.			Date ______
	To ______			From ______
	By ______			By ______

TO: All units

Sender's Number.	Day of Month	In reply to Number	AAA
*B.M. 730	15th		

Brigade	will	move	this	afternoon
to	new	billeting	area	AAA
All	parades	cancelled	AAA	Blankets
will	be	collected	and	stored
in	the	theatre	BONNEHEM	
AAA	The	same	men	as
before	will	be	detailed	as
guards	AAA	Lecture	for	junior
officers	is	cancelled.		

From	83rd	Bde	
Place			
Time		1.30	pm

The above may be forwarded as now corrected. ______ *Censor.*

(Z) ______ Signature of Addressor or person authorised to telegraph in his name.

* This line should be erased if not required.

(774-5) —McC. & Co. Ltd., London.— W 1789/1402. 150,000. 8/15. Forms C 2121/10.

"A" Form. Army Form C. 2121.

MESSAGES AND SIGNALS.

No. of Message ....

Prefix .... Code .... m. | Words | Charge

Office of Origin and Service Instructions

Sent
At .... m.
To ....
By ....

This message is on a/c of:

.... *Service.*

(Signature of "Franking Officer.")

Recd. at .... m.
Date ....
From ....
By ....

TO

Sender's Number	Day of Month	In reply to Number	AAA
*			

directly	it	is	taken	AAA
1/York	and	Lancaster	Regt	will
move	up	to	hold	the
front	British	line	as	it
is	vacated	by	2nd	East
Yorks	and	1/KOYLI	AAA	Suffolk
Regt	will	be	in	support
trenches	behind	1st	York	and
Lancs	Regt	AAA	2nd	E.
Surrey	Regt	will	be	at
Central	Keep	in	reserve	

From 83 Bde
Place
Time 1.45 am

The above may be forwarded as now corrected.

.... *Censor.*

(Z) Lt. R.S. Follett [illegible]

Signature of Addressor or person authorised to telegraph in his name.

* This line should be erased if not required.

(15491) S. & Co. Ltd. W 14142/611. 90,000. 1/15. Forms C 2121/10.

www.ingramcontent.com/pod-product-compliance
Lightning Source LLC
Chambersburg PA
CBHW081422160426
43193CB00013B/2173
9781474514200